W9-BYL-401

River Teeth Literary Nonfiction Prize

SERIES EDITORS:
Daniel Lehman, *Ashland University*
Joe Mackall, *Ashland University*

The River Teeth Literary Nonfiction Prize is awarded to the best work of literary nonfiction submitted to the annual contest sponsored by *River Teeth: A Journal of Nonfiction Narrative.*

The World Before Mirrors

JOAN CONNOR

University of Nebraska Press | Lincoln and London

The author has fictionalized names
and events in the collection.

© 2006 by the Board of
Regents of the University of Nebraska
All rights reserved
Manufactured in the United States
of America ⊗

Library of Congress
Cataloging-in-Publication Data
Connor, Joan.
The world before mirrors / Joan Connor.
p.   cm.—(River teeth literary nonfiction prize)
ISBN-13: 978-0-8032-6455-7 (pbk.: alk. paper)
ISBN-10: 0-8032-6455-0 (pbk.: alk. paper)
I. Title.   II. River teeth literary nonfiction prize (Series)
PS3553.O514255W67   2006
814'.54—dc22
2005029667

Set in Minion by Bob Reitz.
Designed by A. Shahan.

To the great state of Vermont and Norman, my love.

Contents

Acknowledgments

"Sleeping with Thurber" and "Masque" first appeared in *Under the Sun*. "My Son at Thirteen" appeared in *The Heartlands Today*; "The Waiting Room" in *River Teeth*; "Forsaken Places" in *The Mid-American Review*; "The World Before Mirrors" in *The Gettysburg Review*; "Bone Key" in *The Black Warrior Review*; "Abandoned Shoe" in *Terra Incognita*; and "Tolstoy's Daughter" in *The Connecticut Review*. Some of the essays appeared in slightly different versions.

The author wishes to thank Clint McCown for the phrase in the title essay and title.

Sleeping With Thurber

I was raised on Thurber the way most kids were raised on Maypo. On Sunday drives, on cross-country camping trips, my mother read aloud to us. While reading *The Night the Ghost Got In* or *The Bed Broke*, she started laughing, laughing so hard that she cried, that she choked, that she dropped the book. Laughter tutored me in Thurber. The escalating mayhem of family life was our modus operandi. We found ourselves in the baffled predicaments of Thurber's pages.

When we were children, my parents owned a series of vw bugs. One of us would have to sit in the way-back, a luggage cubby. I can still feel the burlap roughness of the fabric, the air swirling in from the sunroof when I read Thurber today. He still is one of the few writers who can make me laugh out loud. He is family. He is a Sunday drive and a scratchy fabric rubbing me raw.

Family. One Thanksgiving we were all in our various wings and bays of the Victorian queen we called home for a time in western New York. (Like Thurbers, we were peripatetic.) My grandmother was in the living room, keeping herself busy whistling for the dog and caning him on the cranium when he complied, tying towlines to his tail so that the cat would shadow him, pouncing. By the pocketa-thockata, I knew that someone was in the poolroom, probably some of my brothers' friends.

My older brother was wheezing away at the pump organ, some lugubrious unrecognizable tune. From the kitchen, the rising smell of rising dough and clanging pot lids, located my mother. My younger brother and the dementos of his Mad Scientists Club were banging a proto-robot, Robbie, into the hall walls. My father was in his study. One could only know this by his habit to be in his study; he was a quiet man during the holiday invasion. I was sewing, alternately altering and trying on clothes before the armoire mirror. Hems crawling up, waists and legs, pegging in.

Such was the domestic scene when the entire house fell dark, dark on us and all of our various occupations, which shuddered to a silence, eerily trailed by an attenuated chord from the organ. "So?" the house asked. And then one thin, high voice wafted in a quaver from the parlor, "Where was Moses when the lights went out?" And in darkness, the house laughed, all of us laughing from our arrested enterprises here, there, and thither. Even my father poked his head out of his study. I knew then that we were a Thurber family.

But I'd known it earlier, too. There was the aunt who saw panthers. The uncle who used to sing "olives" for no particular reason at unprovoked times. The uncle who goosed people and drove a Model T on the sidewalk and wore suspenders and offered his knee to anyone who offered his hand. (He idolized Harpo Marx. He was also senior partner in the family law firm. How many deals were shaken on and shaken?) Another uncle who would, impromptu, recite poetry much to the befuddlement of storekeepers who failed to see the connection between *wandering lonely as a cloud*, say, and purchasing a bag of feed. He was given to epic recollection of stanzas at a moment's notice, frequently the wrong one.

When we laughed at Thurber, we did not laugh at his exaggeration but at his understatement. We did not laugh at the oddness of his characters but at their familiarity — much as we laughed at our own family members. An affectionate laugh of bemusement and an unexpressed, slightly queasy, hope that *this* was as far as things were going to go.

When we lived in Vermont, the aunts and uncles used to get together and read aloud. The cousins shared two rooms, dormitory-style, on the second floor. After being dispatched to sleep, we'd sneak out of bed, hunker down over the heating grate, and peep through its curlicued iron at our increasingly inebriated theatrical family. One version of *Juno and the Paycock* got us found out, because one uncle was delivering Johnny's lines with a singsong Swedish accent that soon had the five of us rolling with insuppressible stomach clutches. "Hooly Moothher-a o' God-a." Flumpty, flumpty, flumpty.

The grate closed, shades drawn, lights snapped off, and hall door shut, we were soon whispering giggles in the dark. We were familiar to ourselves, but we knew that we were an odd lot.

One of book reviewers' and interviewers' favorite questions is : who are your favorite writers? Or the alternate: who are your authorial influences? Thurber always makes my list. When I name him, I usually receive an incredulous, "Really? Thurber?" Yes, really, Thurber. But I know the source of skepticism. Feminist critics regard him as misogynist; others as racist. He is, as I read him, neither. His war between men and women, he simply reported from the front, the trenches, his personal battlefield: Eva, Minette, Althea, Ann, Helen. And the maids with their dialects were not the butt of Thurber's humor, but rather its wielders. They held him in thrall with a private argot which he could not decipher even with *Fowler's* in hand. He has slipped from literary scrutiny, I think, because he is funny, and ours is not a funny age. Ours is the Iron Age, the age of the arched eyebrow and facile satiric detachment. We could do with more wit. Despair is easy, and irony is cheap.

Last summer I slept in Thurber's room, beneath his red and white patchwork quilt, on his single Spartan bed. I stared in his mirror, expecting to see his owlish image wavering in the silvered back. I used the brush in his kit bag. I bathed in his claw-footed tub. With the permission of the director of Thurber House, I even pounded on the old Underwood's keys at Thurber's desk. The keys were recalcitrant—aerobic typing. On a card, I hand-wrote "I am typing on Thurber's Underwood," then typed, "See?" and sent the card to my former lover. But he didn't see. I, however, did.

I saw. Seesaw. *My love is like a see saw,* so Aretha sings. I came. I saw. I left. Veni. Vidi. And wee wee wee all the way home. That was our three-day weekend at the B and B. I am heir to Thurber's general uneasiness around the opposite gender. It's not that I don't like men; I simply have begun to conclude tenuously that we are disparate species. Perhaps it isn't gender, however; it may be that the world divides into those who hear seals bark and those who don't. I am decidedly in the category of those who hear seals bark, but I fall in love with people who do not hear seals bark and do not fall in love with people who do hear seals bark. But I hear seals bark and mermaids sing. And, yes, they sing to me. I eat peaches by the bushel. I am one who hears seals bark and sees spooks haunt.

Thurber believed that the house at 77 Jefferson was haunted. If he believed, I believed. At Thurber House for a reading in 1998, my secondary motivation was to see a ghost, preferably Thurber's. I did not want my bed to break, but I did want the ghost to get in. And one, of sorts, obliged. My prep-school boy-friend attended the reading, someone whom I had not seen since 1971. Twenty-seven years accumulate on people differently. I'd been sad about my life recently, but seeing him made me ecstatic. (Cruel as the confession may be.) We had two drinks, and I returned to sleep at Thurber House. But I did not sleep. I gloated about how swell my life was—relatively. And I listened for the creaks and clunks that could signify a ghost, but the house was still, as still as the typewriter on which I had typed the short note to a man who could not love me. *See?* But so much passes unseen.

Thurber lived in this haunted house from 1913 to 1917. He was attending OSU then and acquiring the experiences which would become *My Life and Hard Times.* Houses take on the character of people who live in them. Thurber was happy here, I sense. It's in the whimsy of the parlor papers, their coziness, the stained light filtering on the staircase, the long windows in his bedroom, the elegant mantel of his fireplace, his Underwood overseeing the small desk. And electricity is leaking all over the house; I felt it in my forearm hairs. He was happy here.

We do not, I suspect, know the moment of our happiness as we live it. Mine was when the man who does not see took my hand while he was driving, took my hand as if he had concluded something, took my hand as if it were something that he wanted to hold onto. I did not know where we were going, but I loved his touch, for that instant, in the car, on some back road in Vermont, where we were then in some unnamed town, neither here nor there.

Nowhere now, I still would not erase that instant despite all the unhappiness that happy moment purchased later. This is how we live in time—our futures becoming themselves, passing to haunt our own pasts.

Thurber's quilt is red and white, double-diamond, topstitched with snowflakes. Red and white are merry colors, the colors of holiday, fairy tale; primitive colors, red blood of hymen, menstruation, birth, death, and white of semen. Red and white are the colors of cards. The jack of hearts, the knave of hearts.

Thurber was happy here, beneath this quilt, reading Henry James, idealizing his women who could not finally support his romantic notions. Perhaps all love fails because of some implicit ideal. But he was happy then, happy in that blind notion of womanhood. *See?* No.

Not sleeping at Thurber House, I tried to re-conjure my prep-school boyfriend. He was small then, a runner. He had a trust fund, a huge LP collection, and bags of dope. Today he is round. He works for the phone company. He rarely buys CDs. He never drinks more than two beers.

And the man who doesn't see? He (like I) has not much changed over the years. We are contours, like Thurber's cartoons, not shape-shifters in size, but shape-shifters both within, becoming strange to ourselves and others. But his contours gave my love a shape for a while. His thighs are heartbreaking, his tree-trunk thighs; and his eyes, his troubled eyes. They are my own. This failed love, this, too, is mine. My heart is held together like the state of Vermont with duct tape and barbed wire. But I crawl along, a shell-less turtle.

A week ago, a week before I read at Thurber House, we were together in a yellow room with a pencil-post bed. The shadow of a bedpost crosses the naked body of a woman like a gnomon. "No man," Odysseus identified himself.

And I love "no man." This seems to be my quest's path, to love no man although I have loved them all, and one specifically from whom I could bloom with no more than a touch. But the knave of hearts . . . And all the tarts are gone, my sweet.

As Alice said, We are just a deck of cards. But flimsy as we are, we crave hearts and faces, Janus-headed, in profile staring at the future and the past. Shuffle, just shuffle, and preferably not off to Buffle. Diamonds: might I not have just one, Ace? But I fold before you raise me. I'm such a card.

Thurber loved wordplay, especially in the dim, declining years. Words jouncing and bouncing around in his unsighted mind. As I do not sleep beneath his quilt, I think of Jamie rhyming and writing away his boredom or railing and reeling drunk through the hallways of his anger, setting fire to his buildings. Castrated, his old eyes. Roaring blind like Oedipus. We all gouge out our eyes, hellbent on unseeing, unriddling the Sphinx.

All night I do not sleep in Thurber's bed. At six in the morning, I catch a taxi to the airport. I need a laugh. Thurber defined humor as "emotional chaos recollected in tranquility." It may be, too, emotional tranquility recollected in chaos. Both are funny on the page; neither in a life. Just a week ago I was in a B and B with the man who cannot see. It was a quiet three days that threw me later for a loop, a loop-de-loop in the loopholes of loving. Later, he did not call. Tranquility recollected in emotional chaos. It is funny in a sad way. Truly funny people are always serious at heart because they know that life is the diminishing circle at the end of a cartoon, Charlie Chaplin's tramp tramping down the road. The receding back. I am an expert at receding backs.

Wordplay and wit are my versions of despair. It is tough work to laugh, tougher to be happy than to be sad. Happy is active; despair is passive. They are the same emotion when they merge: passion.

Narrative discourse and time. Deictics. In this essay, the past keeps insisting on becoming present. It is present in my heart. Missing someone you love is the phantom pain of an amputated limb. I still talk to the man who does not see. He is in my cells; his swallowed come reconstituted in me. So I talk to myself, to the him in me. Years ago I used to talk to my dog; she had no sense of irony but perfect clarity of understanding. When she died, I kept talking, and my family members knew that I'd been talking to myself for years. Perhaps we are always talking to ourselves, old geezers mumbling into our golf pants. The past like an altered old flame keeps showing up at readings, nervously asking for a chair, introducing himself, reintroducing himself. That is the nature of memory.

In grammar, this slide in time as past becomes "now," "then," "here," "there," "today" is: deictics. Literally, deictic means to show directly. My love prefers to show directly. Its opposite, elenctic, means: serving to refute. The man who does not see prefers his love elenctic. What is the proof of love? Is it in time, delay, endless deferral or here, now, there, today? When you love someone, he, like Chickenman, is everywhere. The anti-Superhero, he observes no geography or time. *See?* No. Emily Dickinson wrote, "Absence is compressed presence." It feels like that.

I worry that love's unattainability may be what makes it love. That it is what (or whom) we can't have that leaves us wanting. Wanting as desire: wanting as lack. I think of Thurber idealizing Eva, longing for Honeycutt, ending with Helen guiding him by the elbow as he dropped ashes on his trouser leg and peered, blind, through his spectacles. And how will I end—alone, feeling my way down the wall, making a spectacle of myself but lacking an audience? We want our wanting.

At the end, Thurber raged at Helen, contemned her for helping him in his inadequacy because, perhaps, it made him aware of it. We cannot bear much guidance, much help, much love and how they confer on us knowledge of our shortcomings, our dependence on an other, even an other who is no longer present.

But back in time, in prep school, I welcomed the boyfriends, invited them all. Groping gives us hope. We keep looking for the dependence which we cannot bear. When I was younger, it was more bearable.

Earlier in the summer, before the weekend at the B and B, before the reading at Thurber House, my family had a memorial service for my uncle, the one who recited poetry impromptu. At sunset I watched the newest generation of my relatives, all strange to me, drink and eat and joke and flirt. I do not even know their names; they no longer resemble my memories of them. My family used to get together for Fourth of July picnics on lawns surrounded by primroses, columbines, and nodding phlox. Now we get together for funerals, and, soon, we will not get together at all. This is my family of strangers, scattered over the continent. Children of first cousins and second, dandelions gone to seed.

But at sunset we walked up the pasture to the rock outcropping. Purple clouds bellied like whales on the ring of mountains, backlit red by the dipped sun. The hush was like dew in the field that my uncle used to hay. I watched the beautiful grandchildren, slim, somber, very young, younger than they knew, toss scoops of my uncle's ashes into the wind, and they spumed over the field in the chill still. This was an elegy for a man who recited poetry while pitching hay.

A generation before mine, my mother and her friends had hayrides here in the summer. At Thanksgiving we ground up Teer Road on the tractor to harvest our Christmas trees on the fringes of this pasture. Underneath it, a cave gapes, a cave which the farmer, who used to take my mother on hayrides, filled in, fearing that the children might be swallowed.

My brothers and I used to explore this field, excavating for the hollow, or sinkhole that might be the entrance to the cave. For several summers, we lived in the cabin at the edge of the field. The cabin smelled of gas from the stove, kerosene from the lamps, mothballs, and sulfur matches, old board games and older books. At night, we huddled outside with the uncles and aunts and cousins and sang faulty harmonies to *Down by the Old Mill Stream*, to banjo and guitar accompaniment, occasionally a harmonica, around a spitting fire in the huge iron cauldron. This Vermont my son will never know because the family is scattered now.

But I like thinking of the cave beneath the field, the cave that we never found. It is there like memory, our family's collective memory, a less willful consciousness. We become terrain.

What we do not find, what we hide, or what hides from us informs the life that we lead above. Concealed, it nonetheless abides. The dark, blind chambers of the heart. Always there is something more, something unseen, the unlived life, the underworld in us. *See?* No.

The unknown members of my family, the strangers, they, too, all carry this strangeness: their misplaced loves, their aspirations to be painters and filmmakers and historians, their disappointments, and it all goes unseen, maybe unsaid.

Now that I am a professor, I have my uncle's library on my shelves. He used to be a Dartmouth English professor; he retired to write, never becoming the poet, perhaps, or the scholar whom he wanted to be; he became beloved, however, by his grandchildren who came to his hilltop farm to ride tractors and feed chickens and pitch hay. Love. That's a life's work.

I used to go to my aunt and uncle's house. Classical music sifted like sun into the airy rooms, soup simmered on the cookstove, my uncle read, my aunt worked in her art studio. They could not know this, but I decided on these visits that this was the life I wanted—calm, creative, thoughtful. And I have achieved that life—or nearly. I never found their partnership, their love for each other. I have the life but not the partner. Middle-aged and alone, I am puzzling now what meaning a bluebird has when you spot it on the mailbox and there is no one to tell. I have not seen bluebirds in many years. I have one now in my yard in Ohio. Its blueness startles. When my son gets off the school bus, I tell him, but he does not know the meaning of a bluebird on a mailbox, how they once spotted Vermont in the summers, how they are no longer there, how here in Ohio they arrive like manifestations of memory. Mine. But I like to think that I might yet meet someone who knows the significance of a bluebird on a mailbox.

My son rides a *Bluebird* bus. It may be enough. There are many qualities of love. Family. My love arrives in a tie-dyed T-shirt and oversized jeans, tripping on his sneaker laces as he descends the steps of the *Bluebird* bus. It is as good as a bluebird in Vermont.

But can a poem, or an essay, or a story compensate for love of another quality? I still do not know, but it is where I divert my energy. Blind, Thurber could recite entire essays by memory. That is a form of love. But I see. See? No. Not even by the antique keys of Thurber's Underwood, underworld.

On the way home from the memorial service, one of the uncles told an anecdote. The Algonquin Club used to descend in the summers on Neshobe, Alexander Wolcott's summer estate, an island in Lake Bomoseen in Vermont. One summer, fresh from *The King and I,* Gertrude Lawrence, muffled in furs, waltzed into my Great-aunt May's antique store in Belmont, Vermont, accompanied by Harpo Marx. Talk about a misturn. Back then the roads in town were all dirt roads and unmapped. Harpo Marx in Belmont, Vermont: a definition of surrealism. Aunt May was strict Yankee stock, not one to put up with any antics. Hawk-eyed and unamused, she endured Harpo as he riffled through her stock of antique bottles and old linens and postcards. She had no time for New York women wearing fur in summer. (That violated a dual taboo: women from New York, and women who didn't know that furs never, but never, ever came out of dry storage before the period between Thanksgiving and Christmas.)

Laughing, Lawrence and Marx left without making a purchase. The women in my family are formidable, and I suspect that Yankee May knew that their nonsense was at her expense, that they regarded her as quaint and as obsolete as one of her own antiques, a bedwarmer or a yarnwinder. She was not about to participate in their mockery. (After all, there were rules about New York floozies and fur-wearing to uphold.) The antique store, although it is no longer an antique store, still stands. The remaining aunts today oversee the historical society. There is a photograph of Aunt May in the archives. Memory pertains as long as we don't forget it.

A friend told me that Neshobe means *mosquito.* I take it on faith; I cannot know if the translation is accurate. But I've no doubt that Aunt May dispatched the two off to their island enclave of New Yorkers with the same grim glee with which she'd swat a Neshobe, mistranslated or not.

The uncle who told me the anecdote emulated Harpo Marx. Thurber adored him. They shared a genius for silliness. Although Aunt May would not approve, I too love mischief, the stray thought, the silly. My mind, like Thurber's is all *usher,* but I respect Aunt May for her fortitude and my uncle for telling the story. Had he not, it would have been lost forever, and I would not know that I had this connection with Thurber, Thurber's circle, however oblique the connection. Thurber:Harpo:Aunt May.

The most significant connections are often the flimsiest. The perhaps of metaphor, the carom of a glance, a bluebird on a mailbox, a time-worn red and white quilt, an unanswered letter, asking *See?* They clutter our antique stores, hollow our ground with subterranean longing, fill our caves with want. But, want, too, is something and is preferable to nothing. Absence become presence in the deictic of our loving or our having loved. Want colors in the contours of our cartoons.

Last night was a full moon. The world was yellow, yellow like wolves' tapeta, and I was sleepless again. On full moons, I always think of him, the one who doesn't see. It raises the tide of longing, the awareness of time passing through its cycles, but the cycles do not change. Even at new moon, when there is no light, there is still a moon. Love is like that. I felt electricity leaking all over the universe, and then the dogs began. One dog at first. A neighbor's. A small, fat, overbred black Lab. A single barking at shadows. Then another dog, and another, fugal dogs ululating at the moon. What atavistic memory motivated them back into a pack, what longing raised their voices to sing down the moon? I, too, howl at moons. And then, suddenly, coda. The mournful music stopped. Frosty air, the dew crestfallen, growing crunchy on the grass. I stared out my window at the moon spilling over the stubbled Ohio field where ghosts tiptoed toward Halloween. The same moon shines on him in Maine where a seal barks. And I hear it.

When I was married, I used to sail in Casco Bay with my husband and the dog who listened. Once, dog in the bow, we pulled up alongside a bell buoy where a fat seal lolled. Brown eyes to brown eyes, dog snuffled seal, and seal snuffled dog, whiskers twitching. My dog quivered. They held each other like that for a while. The seal barked. The dog barked. They recognized each other. But one lived above and the other below. That is how I love him. He fins and swims beneath my surface. I am out of my element.

This is my memorial service for Thurber, and for my uncle, and Aunt May (whom I never met), and for an earlier incarnation of the prep-school boyfriend, for my canine confidante, and the futures of my unknown second and third cousins and their children, and for him, the one who cannot see. For all the anecdotes never recounted and buried in legendary caves. Perhaps these will be the stories that I one day recount to my son or grandchild, my version of the anecdote of the antique store. Through these connections, missed connections, or misconnections of memory, someone will begin to see. Our lives and hard times. Loving is hard time. But consider the alternative. Intelligence, seeing, is a curse and a blessing; we presume that we see. But we see so little. So much lingers or lurks in the caves within. But consider the alternative. Our memories. We take them with us, or we offer them. I offer these. For my uncle. To my son. To him.

My Son at Thirteen

The year that my son taught me to fly was an otherwise unre-
markable year. I was waiting. I do not know for what. Perhaps
to learn to fly. But I was waiting, living in Ohio, the state before
grace, where I had followed a job if not my heart. Homesick
and lovesick for a man who had forgotten me states and years
ago, I filled time applying for jobs and reading atlases, mapping
routes into unlikely hope and an uncertain future. The shortest
distance between two points is hope. And hope is not a straight
line. Geography can be destiny.

Dating was out of the question. My son, Norman, had devel-
oped an uncanny if cruel knack for impersonation. As I greeted
my date du jour at the door, I'd dread turning around and
glimpsing some impish skit. For some mysterious reason, I'd
had a run of limpers and would catch Norm dragging his leg like
a corpse with *Creature Feature* glee as I halfheartedly answered
the doorbell.

I got tired of responding to delicate questions about Norman's limp while I avoided posing my own about my dates'. ("So,
Gimpy, how'd you get the bum leg?") Charley horses galloped

through the paddocks of awkward conversations in overlong rides to and from mediocre restaurants. Ohio, where they eat but do not dine. Ohio, when you order salad, you get iceberg. It sank the Titanic.

It became easier to stay home. Norm did voices as well as gaits, voices so accurate that they could make me spin around, anticipating Norm's father, or my mother, or the man who had forgotten me. Norman picked them up immediately, in any register, cartoon or actual, male or female. He could even mimic specific neighborhood dogs' bays, yips, and howls. And mine of course. Norm echoed my repertoire of barks and voices so precisely that I'd wonder, just for a shiver of time, if I'd spoken, or mumbled, yapped, or hmmm'ed. Then he grinned. Despite the mite of meanness in his mischief, he made me laugh. We needed to laugh. It was the motive for his mimicry. Laughter was the quickest way out of Ohio.

And we played games. Neither Norman nor I will read a manual. We are impatient with directions but impulsive in action. So we plunged into this interminable, impenetrable game, which he was keen on at the time, involving wars and battles and evolving characters and dynamo cards, which pitched us both into edgy hysterical laughter just this side of panic.

"You can't challenge me with that Enchanto-lizard; he's not evolved," Norman said.

"Then evolve him."

"You can't just evolve him. You need a dynamo card."

"Okay, how do I get a dynamo card?"

"I don't know. Read the rules."

"You read the rules." While Norman pouted, I'd steal some of his jewels, these pretty parti-colored pebbles of glass whose function in the game eluded us, but at least they were pretty to look at, pretty to hold. Pretty to hoard.

Norman would pretend to read the game rules manifesto for a paragraph or two before he noticed the missing jewels. "Hey."

"I stole them. Ha ha, I win."

For a moment, Norman would laugh at my perverseness before muttering through tears of frustration, "You're not taking this seriously."

"It's a *game.*"

"You could try."

"I'm not evolved."

Then Norman would toss the cards all over the carpet, signaling the end of the game and our mutual relief.

Which is not to say that I didn't learn from the game. I did. A great deal. I learned that the problem with the dates wasn't really the limps or Norman's improv theater. It was a problem of evolution.

One of my dates, Limpy the First, told me raucously funny stories over dinner about getting bashed and mooning his colleagues at a recent conference. Another, Limpy Redux, told me about a recent date of his who asked him if he'd like to pet her iguana. His riposte: if that's what you want to call your *down there,* I'll pet it. Har de har.

Bare butts and pussy jokes didn't strike me as first-date fare. But what did I know? Truth was: I was unevolved, too—stuck in Ohio, stuck in love with someone who did not, could not love me. Simply: I fell in love and couldn't fall back out. There is no manual for falling out of love, no exit sign shimmering red light over the long, white-tiled floor of the hall. Stuck. "Stuck," as my former lover wrote me in one of his last letters to me. "It's not a good place to be, but at least you know where you want to be."

I knew where I wanted to be—unstuck. But there was no going back. I was not wanted there, and it was five years ago. Time marched on, but place had a tendency to stay in place even while continents navigated lava seas. There was still home, Back East, capitalized in my landlocked imagination. But the job applications and road maps were not cooperating. Stuck. Unevolved and all the semiprecious glass gravel in Ohio would not buy me a ticket out. I felt like a hand groping a dark hall wall for a light switch. Toggle on. Please, on. Waiting. Waiting because I believed this: love does not shift tense. I loved: I love. And I knew where home was. Not here. I was in my forties and still learning how to walk. A limper myself.

One of my former lover's last lines to me: I don't need this anymore. That much was self-evident; it's all a question of which word bore the stress.

I cried. My eyelids were so swollen that I had to put hemorrhoid cream on them in order to insert my contacts. I don't need *that* anymore.

But still we remained in touch, the occasional e-mail, two blips who passed in the night, and I spent insomniac nights in Ohio speaking to him on the edge of dreams. My computer had a sleep mode; why didn't I?

Norman took to designing his own interminable games, spending hours with paintbrushes configuring his labyrinthine boards, extorting money from the Monopoly game to dole out to the imagined players. With toothpicks, he raised elaborate castles with turrets and parapets. With snarls of thread and common pins, he forested topiary copses. With the salvaged glass pebbles, he paved roads and pathways. On index cards, he penned and painted creatures grotesque and lovely, benign and malign, elaborating in a careful, cribbed script their attributes and powers. He carved miniature statues from seashell soaps and installed them among the topiary, slung Origami cranes on fishing filament. And he cut out and designed an ingenious pit, labeled The Hollows, but to which no paths led. On the seventh day, he rested before summoning me to play.

We rolled his hand-dotted sugar cube dice and we moved space forward, space back, following the carefully lettered, minute instructions in the squares along the paths and by-paths for one hour, two, before I realized that this game, too, was going nowhere. The game was objectless. For all its beauty, its intricate detail, its meticulous painstaking lavishment of art and time, it was pointless. The object of the game was the game. There was no way to win, no way to end but to end.

For a byway or two past the realization, I bided my time, prodded my game piece, a horned otter, and nipped my impatient tongue until my mouth watered with iron, rust. "Um," I said. I picked at a ruby paving stone with my crescent fingernail. (Ohio left much time for assiduous manicure. On a good Saturday, I could file a nail to the nub and buy myself some time to watch it re-grow.) "What's the point?"

My voice flew back at me in perfect pitch. "What's the point?" I nodded.

Norman nodded. He did facial expressions, too. I scrutinized mine, seeing it as Norman wore it, as he must see it. What I saw made me sad. A mask with all the pizzazz of a caged orangutan in November sitting on a bunch of bruised bananas while fruit flies listlessly battered his eyes. Mange of the soul. I was what happened when bananas went bad. Hoodlum fruit with hooded eyes hanging out with bruised skin, emanating a too-sweet decay. But maybe it was Norman's expression after all. It altered suddenly. He squinted at me.

"The point?"

"Point." Yes. I nodded.

"Never mind. If you have to ask, you'll never get it."

"There are no rules," I said.

"There are directions." He pointed one of his nibbled fingernails at one of the inscribed squares.

"It's not the same thing. No rules, no one can win."

Norman nodded, but the nod wanted to be a shake. Again he said, "Never mind," and he kneeled and rolled the game, still unnamed, into a tube of poster board. All the architecture, all the creatures, all the cards and cranes, and fantastic forests Norman rolled inside with a solemnity peculiar to thirteen-year-old boys who live alone with their dateless mothers who refuse to read manuals in Ohio.

Once when the man who could not love me said, "I don't get you," I said, "Nobody *gets* anyone. There are no guidelines. There are no rules."

He said, "That's just easy nihilism."

I said, "Nihilism is never easy. It's hard work, nihilism. I mean, it's depressing."

Nihilism was the wrong word. Anarchy was the mot juste. Love is anarchic.

Norman did not invite me to play again, and I did not ask. Although I do not read manuals in Ohio or anywhere else, I do use every second of time to a purpose. I mend while I watch television. I read while I sunbathe. I lift weights while I listen to the radio. I manicure my finger-nubs on endless dateless Saturdays, balance bipolar checking accounts. I cannot live without an objective. This may be why I do not read manuals; it gives me a chance to fill time by figuring out how machines and furniture and numbers work, how they are assembled, or filled in—or how they should have been. It explains, too, why much of my furniture and arithmetic are inventive or wobbly. I have scrabbled together tables and magazine racks and sums and meanings. At least there is a significance, a purpose, dangling out there somewhere, waiting to be solved. Waiting. Waiting games.

When Norman was six he reached across the dinner table and grabbed my hand, sobbing.

"Honey, " I said, "what's wrong?"

"I just realized that you are going to die."

Uh oh. I tried to console him. Then he glanced up at me, tearless now, with a Hey-wait-just-a-minute look. The slow dawn. "Am I going to die, too?"

That is how it begins. Waiting games.

A colleague told me recently that caged birds get hysterical at dusk. They do not think that the day is ending but that the world is ending. That is why pet owners cover their cages. I do not know how she knows this. How does one know what an uncovered bird thinks? Chicken Little, the sky is falling. Does a bird have sufficient bird-brain to conceptualize apocalypse? What is a bird Armageddon? Four cats on horseback? A mongoose with appetite of legend? And how would one know exactly that a bird was hysterical? The emotional range of canaries seems as small as their dollop of feathered flesh: peck, flap, trill. Molt at will? But it had a tinny, pet-toy ring of truth: enclose a small darkness to ward off the immensity of darkness encroaching slinkily, cat-like on its fog-padded feet from every quarter. That, I believed.

The last image I have of the man who could not love me is of him in a parking lot. He is wearing sunglasses and waving. A wave: the perfect ambiguous gesture. It means hello. It means good-bye. I would like to believe that it was ambiguous, but I know which he meant. The last time that I fell in love I knew that it was the *last time*. And the last time that I saw him, I knew that it was the *last* time. We cover the cages.

With the games securely closeted, Norman began disassembling his action figures and rebuilding them into creatures of his own devising. Norman: a serial resurrector set. His playroom looked like a used body parts store, with heaps of cannibalized light chains and wings and plastic arms and legs, rolls of tape and squished tubes of superglue, model paints and scavenged bits of jewelry, fliptops, and bent paper clips. The new army of action figures he endowed with supernatural powers. Day-Glo griffins with savage teeth who could ice their adversaries, winged dogs who salivated spears, chicken-legged rabbits who pecked their opponents senseless, then hopped on. "This one can move in and out of Ohio at will," he said, holding out a Stega-unicorn-asaurus.

I studied him to see if he was teasing me, but Norman's face reflected more than it revealed. I beheld my own puzzlement. It pleased him. He grinned, no longer toothily, the adverb which would have applied when we first moved here and he was eight years old.

He glanced up at me, waiting. When I said nothing, he said, "You give me a lot to worry about." I did not know what he meant, but I nodded. My son at thirteen.

Around this time Norman began speaking in aphorisms. *No one can foretell the future. You and men don't mix.* He would deliver these little dicta with serious eyes and gnomic intonations, usually popping around a corner, then pausing to adopt a dramatic stance. It gave me the willies. I began to feel as if I were cohabiting with some teenaged nail-biting Tiresias. *Inner peace is truly inner.*

His father had favored the adage, too, but his had run more to cliché. *You'll catch more flies with honey than vinegar.* But who wanted flies?

One evening while I was reading on the loveseat and filing my ring fingernail, Norman bustled into the kitchen, all business like a cat that suddenly gets a bolting notion: places to go, people to see, out of my way. I'm a busy, busy cat.

Norman hunched over the junk drawer, clawing furiously. Bag ties, plastic lids, glue bottles, and screwdrivers spewed and arced.

"What are you doing?" I asked, watching the news network recycle the headlines—market up, temperatures down, starving babies, humanitarian bombing.

Each man should mind his own hands.

"Norman, what are you doing?"

"I'm building something. Do we have any small leather jackets?"

"Any what?"

"Small leather jackets." Norman stopped ferreting and cocked his arm, tilted his head, and gave me the What-are-you?-An Andromedan? look.

"No." I stopped filing. "Not a single tiny leather jacket left. Stuart Little and his gang of mini-thugs hopped on their hawgs and cycled on." Norman did not laugh. I considered his angular posture. "What, exactly, are you building?"

"An action figure."

"Why do you need a small leather jacket?"

"Do you have any leather then?"

"I have some elbow patches, but they're suede. In the sewing basket."

Norman disappeared into the dining room.

"But why do you need to make a small leather jacket?" I called.

"I am making an action figure of me."

"You are making a Norman action figure?"

"Not just Norman. *Ab*-nor-man. He looks like me, but he has great abs and can roll with any body punch you deliver. He's like me, only super." And he banged upstairs, I assumed with the elbow patches once intended for my tweed jacket to be sewn on during one of my news-junkie junkets. Norman was already super; he didn't need a doppelganger action toy to prove it.

I named him Norman because I knew that life was tough, and I wanted him to be a conqueror. But names are not destiny. Norman was not a conqueror but a quester, an imaginer, a maker of fantastic worlds, a pronouncer of maxims. Norman. When I wanted to irritate him, I sang the old song, "Norman, ooh-oo-oo-oo-oo-oo-oo, Norman, my love."

When he wanted to irritate me, he would pronounce on some statement of mine: OPINION, FACT. This was apparently some unit in middle school designed to develop discrimination. "Honey, you're slouching." OPINION. As an irritation strategy, it was expert. "Eat your bouillabaisse." "I'd rather just have a hot dog." "Eat it; it's good for you." OPINION. I wanted to scrag his teacher's scrawny little opinionated chicken neck.

"Norman, there are no opinions. There are no facts. They're

all intermingled. Some facts are just outright lies. Some opinions are just stupidities with bullhorns."

"OPINION," he said.

"Fact," I said. How could I explain facts in a world of Lewinsky and Starr and Whitewater and Waco? Fact, fact, opinion, fact. Duck, duck, goose. Outright lie, egregious misrepresentation, spin, half-truth.

I surrendered. "You win. Factinion," I whispered as he left the room.

Before I moved to Ohio, I was not a news junkie. And before we moved to Ohio, Norman did not construct action figures of himself. I wondered if this was something to worry about.

The tiny leather jacket was not, in itself, an odd request. On Norman's eleventh birthday, I bought him a black leather jacket which he coveted. I recalled reading, back when I was married and living Back East, an article in *The Globe* on St. Valentine's Day which maintained that every middle-aged man secretly wanted a leather bomber jacket. I bought one for my former husband who turned out not to want one secretly or overtly. But when Norman wanted one, I bought it for him because, if ever a kid really needed a leather jacket, Norman was that kid. Norman was sweet. Too much mother, I suspect, not enough father, leather jackets notwithstanding.

Norman was the first to console a teammate who missed a goal. His coach usually appointed him team leader, not because he was adept—Norman was always the last picked when he wasn't leader—but because he was empathetic. Sportsmanship. It would have handicapped a lesser child.

But Norman was full in his sweetness. He was also a worrier, the anxiety manifesting in habits rather than talk. He chewed his nails, chawed them, gnawed and bloody. Better his nails than his stomach.

So I bought Norman a leather jacket. He needed it. By the same logic, I also bought him a set of weights on his twelfth birthday. Hence abs; hence, Ab-nor-man. But I wondered none-theless if building an action figure of one's self was, forgive the pun, the norm.

When I called my mother, ecstatically ensconced Back East, she reassured me, "It's an empowerment fantasy. All kids have them."

Well, maybe. Maybe, had I been Back East, I'd have found her reassurance more reassuring. But I was a worrier, too, and if not a nail-biter, a compulsive Ohioan filer. I mean, how much power does a thirteen-year-old need? I filed a bit more, and I duly admired Ab-nor-man. It did resemble Norman, right down to the hair color and the little leather jacket. But the facial expression belonged to the superhero whom Norman had decapitated—expressive teeth, a clean-your-clock grimace. I filed. I filed.

Norman did not play with Ab-nor-man. He built him a display case from a two-liter plastic bottle. When I cleaned the playroom, I felt Ab-nor-man's squinched bullying stare on me as if I'd blundered into some Stephen King duo-verse, but I stored my anxiety in my red leather manicure case. My approach to child rearing is the same as my approach to gardening. I don't prune or clip. Let them bloom; they tend to rise toward the sun.

At thirteen Norman uncertainly straddled childhood and teenhood, and I felt each gesture, each moment as the potential last one of the former. Norman had decided that I needed to get out more, so we went to a local theater to see some kiddie movie, an extended commercial really, for the game since shelved with our hysteria.

In his self-awareness, Norman had anticipated that he was a little too old to be seeing it, so he was traveling incognito. He'd shucked his usual biker jacket for a tweed hand-me-down (from who knew who) that I'd bought at a thrift shop. And he pulled an Irish cap down over his reflector-face. Scrunching he hustled through the lobby and plopped down in the first row where he'd be least likely to be spotted by a classmate—who, I pointed out would also have to be attending the movie in order to sight him. But Norman remained hunched into his disguise and illogic through the movie.

I sat in the filtered darkness watching the cartoon film—every bit as saccharine and pointless as the game we'd abandoned— feeling wistful, knowing that this was the last kid vid we'd likely see together. I think that Norman knew it, too. His aerobic nail biting and fidgeting belied boredom, our shared characteristic impatience.

But after the movie, sneaking through the lobby, banging out the door, Norman was chatty. Something about a kid at school who kept threatening to beat him up. Norman stopped mid-sentence and grabbed my hand, the gesture a poignant stab.

I had to draw sudden breath. The bladed air of February cut me. I felt with certainty: this was it. The last time that Norman would take my hand.

But then I felt some difference in the gesture. Norman was not entrusting his hand to mine; he was guiding me. "Watch it," he said, pulling me short.

The yellow eyes of a long black car slid before us, its fins disappearing into the dark lot.

"The cautious man lives."

"Fact," I said.

Norman at thirteen. *Norman, my love.*

And he was. When I was Norman's age my mother used to fill the candy dishes with motto hearts near Valentine's Day. I do the same for Norman. I used to believe that the hearts had a sugary gift of prophecy. If you got the one that read *Be Mine,* or *Love You,* or *Hug Me,* love would find you. Not perhaps as misguided or superstitious as it might at first seem. Chance, too, could be a form of prophecy, as likely as any other. Of course this belief failed to explain the random import of *Oh You Kid* or *Daddy-O,* or *Beat Me,* the last having acquired a new connotation, no doubt since its first printing. I imagined these amatory mottos typeset by an affable oaf of a man in a raccoon coat, toting a ukulele. What did the mottos mean to Norman? Did he read them, these outdated slangy hipsterisms from a sweeter time? Norman preferred the lavender hearts with their slightly soapy taste. I favored the brown ones with their root-beery, underground flavor. The last I'd picked out had been blank, no motto at all. Now that was prophecy.

A week after our movie date, I found Ab-nor-man's display case in the recycling bin. I did not discover Ab-nor-man's disposition, but he was gone. I did not mourn his squinchy stare. I didn't miss him at all although I hoped that he'd transmuted into another incarnation, perhaps a horned otter. But the jacket was a more curious disappearance.

Abruptly Norman stopped wearing his biker gear and started preferring the tweed. I didn't ask what it meant, but I was certain that it meant something. Perhaps in some misguided empowering empowerment fantasy of my own, I signed us up for horseback riding classes. I thought that it would be good for Norman—for his sense of confidence, his sense of control—or maybe I just wanted to fill Ohio time. Waiting.

We went riding on Wednesday nights after my classes ended. We picked hooves, adjusted bridles and blankets and saddles. We curried. By starlight in frosty air, Norman and I trotted through the tiny clouds our breaths huffed in the corral. My aunt had raised Morgan horses, and in the animal odor of manure, the clean, safe smell of hay, the medicinal salve of the liniment, I whiffed a metaphor for Back East. I looked forward to the classes with an enjoyment keener than I felt while on Ginger's back. I pretended that we were heading home. At the class, I watched Norman guide Stubby through the barrels.

When he dismounted, the instructor asked him if he wanted to trot.

"No," he said with an energy that was as pure as starlight.

"Why not?"

"I don't trust them."

Fact. We laughed then. A half-hour later Ginger shied and bucked me. I landed hard and limped to the car that night. How had Norman become so wise at thirteen? And I a limper?

Riding a horse was like loving someone. Illusions of control. Delusions of control. You sit on the back of an animal who could kill you on a whim, who outweighs you, outruns you, who, truth to tell, is only humoring you and only for the while. Rein right, rein left, indeed. Gee. Haw. Golly gee and haw, haw. You're on your back and staring at the stars, you ass. Hee haw, haw, haw. Reins are flimsy. Horses get notional. You can break a horse, but when you ride one you know that a horse is never really broken. At any moment its anarchic heart can kick in, kick you off, canter you right out of the saddle. Why do we get up, dust off our hurt knees, climb back in the saddle again? You cannot break a horse but, yes, a heart. Hi ho, Silver.

Driving home with the radio on, we heard this weather report: *and now a few temperatures around the area: 60, 59, 58.*

I am not making this up.

I did not think that Norman was listening. He said, "And now for the sports update. Here are the scores: 99 to 1, 48 to 47, 3 to 0. And you heard it here live."

I laughed so hard that I hit the windshield wipers thinking that the condensation was outside. I grabbed Norman's hand. He got laughing, too, just for the pure pleasure of pleasing me.

When I caught breath, I said, "What was that?"

"Ohio," he said.

I am or I am not communicating my biases to my son.

I started happily hollering out a song just like Joan Jett. *With my radio on.*

Norman fell quiet for a while, then asked, "Did you ever see that commercial on TV, you know, about how your life doesn't mean anything? Do you ever feel that way?"

Uh oh. I drew a slow breath. If my hands were not on the wheel, I'd hug him.

"Honey, everyone feels that way. Sometimes." But my heart seized. I could hear it in my voice. I am angry that a Dianetics commercial can sadden my son, angry because it poses no solution; there *is* no solution. Angry because my son is thirteen and already sounding out the emptiness at the core of life's drum. Bang the drum dumbly.

"Would you like to go to church?" I asked him.

"No," he said. And he turned his face away from mine watching the dark Appalachian hills gliding by. Coal, clay. Burial mounds. Bad ground.

A personal relationship with God? I suspect that God is too busy keeping the sky from falling for personal relationships. Running a universe is 24–7 and no more Sundays off. Not even Christmas.

My first year in Ohio I spent Christmas alone. I could not afford to fly Back East. Norman was with his dad. I pretended, without success, that it wasn't Christmas. To fend off loneliness I turned on the TV (uncabled then) only to discover that the local channels were wired to the all *Hee Haw* network. Hee haw, hee haw, braying at the stars. Dancing pigs in tutus didn't roast my chestnuts, so I turned on National Public Radio, but it felt very private, too private. Alone, alone, all all alone, alone on a wide blue airwave. I suspected that I was the only human being in radio-land listening to bluegrass Christmas carols. Three bluegrass numbers in a row alter neuro-systems. It's music for hilljack crack addicts. I was a jingle and a jangle bells. Even "Jingle Bell Rock" could have rocked my cradle, soothing me.

I'll have a bluegrass Christmas without you. Snap, snap, snap went the radio. Clang, clang, clang went the trolley of holly. I pretended more mightily that it wasn't Christmas; it was pretense or slit my wrists. The former was less messy.

Norman and I completed the horseback riding class. I recovered from my limp. But I knew that Norman was right. "Don't trust them." Norman started putting scotch tape over his nails so that he wouldn't bite them. "Why?" I asked.

"Something to do."

"But you don't need the tape."

OPINION.

A negative behavior, *not* biting one's nails, something to do? Waiting. Maybe that was life: what happened while you waited for something else to happen.

My son at thirteen.

I was still waiting. On Sundays I watched rerun movies all day while I read the paper. The movies were frequently unintentionally hilarious because of the dubbed lines for home viewers. In *Thelma and Louise,* the wannabe rapist says, "I want you to clean my clock." And she shoots him. KA-pow. It seems an overreaction. After all, who wouldn't prefer a clean timepiece to a dirty one.

"Don't trust them," Norman said.

But I didn't pay attention. I received a call from a man whom Limper the First casually had introduced me to in the restaurant. He wanted to know if I'd like to get together sometime. Never say die. I invited him over to watch a movie.

Things got out of hand or in the wrong hands. Granted the movie, some heroic epic about golf (Golf!) was lousy. Granted he arrived, I whiffed, drunk. But I was unprepared for the tussle, unprepared to find myself splayed, arms pinned, legs pinned like a deer ready for dressing. I suppose that I bleated. I only know this: it was scary. The man was large, outweighed me like a horse its rider. But I was being ridden and couldn't buck him and at that point Norman, supposedly snug abed above stairs, walked in. His presence was enough to do what I could not—remove the lout from my house.

And only at the moment past the door banging, the car starting, the taillights receding, did I cry. Okay, I wept. I sobbed. And

Norman watched all this, not knowing what to do, which made me cry harder, his hands clenching and unclenching helpless at his sides. Then he went upstairs to leave me feeling like a blank motto heart, sobbing, wondering how my life had gone this far amiss. I was better than this; surely I was better than this.

Then Norman was back and in his leather jacket, unrolling the game with no name, and I felt my love for him tauten, stretch, a filament of cranes.

"Do you want to play?" he asked.

Yes, I wanted to play.

So we played, played without the rules in our objectless game, played for the pleasure of it. It was small consolation and just the right amount.

Do not ask me what love is. I will tell you what love is not. It is not horseback riding, or tense shifts (love:loved, a fate accompli). It is not leather jackets or anarchy or nihilism or covered cages or Dianetic Divine Diabetics, or candy hearts in cut-glass dishes. Although it *may* be all these things and more. But it is not these only.

When I stopped crying, Norman said, "It isn't so bad."

I said, "Yes, it is. That's it. That's the last time." And I looked at Norman with his beautiful, worried-boy face, his heart still waiting to be broken.

"No," Norman said, "try this." And he pulled crane from filament and flew it above his world in his fingers, teaching me to fly. "We're getting out of here," he said. "Soaring."

Soar and sore. Homonyms. Saddlesore. Heartsore. Norman was right. We were soaring. We were out of here. We were history, golden.

Do not ask me what love is. If you can answer, you are limping through The Hollows. You will never earn your wings. Never say die. Never say what love is. If you can, ever comes and then you die.

"Fly," Norman said. And then I did, evolving wings without a dynamo card. Fly, fly. And we rose above the topiaries and The Hollows and bad dates with action figures and Ohio and our landlocked sadness there. We were flying home and we never looked back. Not once. Not even for a glimpse. When love shifts tense, prolepsis. Its horizon is future tense and hope restored. We will, Norman. We will.

The past? The present? Ohio? OPINION. OPINION. OPINION. Norman, my love.

The Waiting Room

A man gave me a story to write, but, first, you have to wait.

I am very impatient. But I am expert at waiting. I wait in order not to deal with my impatience. Plots are about withholding, making impatient people wait. If you are no longer waiting, you do not love a plot.

Time makes impatient people wise, however. They do not wait for what will not happen. I am time-wise. I will never be a lingerie model. I will never be a rock star. I do not wait for those futures to happen.

Woody Allen wrote that "most of life is just showing up." That's pretty good. But I think that most of life is waiting. I note, for example, that I spend an inordinate amount of time in waiting rooms.

If I did not show up, if I did not wait, these ob-gyns and car mechanics and orthodontists would bill me by the hour. They have signs announcing this. While they blast their talk shows at me, bliss me out with their lude music, seduce my prurient side with their celebrity magazines, they apparently do not think that I should be billing them for my waiting time.

I am prompt. Punctiliously prompt to a peccadillo of a quarter-hour early. They are running an hour late. There I sit. Do I rant? Do I rave? Do I charge by the billable minute? No. Why? Because beyond the waiting room is the non-waiting room.

The dentist: in Alexandria the dentist has his chalky, stubby, rubbery, latex fingers in your mouth. He says, "Dentistry is a sexual metaphor." His chubby, stubbled cheek is a coarse inch, half-inch from your mouth. You can smell his lunch on his breath; it isn't pleasant.

"Ung," you gurgle with a mouthful of fingers.

"Think about it," he says. "You insert this into that. The mouth, the fingers as metaphor. It's very intimate. An invasion. Think about it."

When one has a mouthful of someone's sausage-stuffed condom fingers, when one has someone drilling and filling, when one can't swallow or breathe and is paying a zillion dollars for the privilege, sexual metaphors are decidedly what one does not want to think about. Sexual metaphors are, in fact, the furthest thing from one's mind. When one is trying to keep a gazillion appliances in one's mouth and divert one's nostrils away from old salami breath, one does not feel sexy at all. Under the best of circumstances, one does not find rape metaphors sexy, and these are not the best of circumstances. One is instead trying to suppress chilling memories of *Marathon Man*. One is not thinking sexily about Nazi dentists with delusions about their patients' digit envy. One is, rather, waiting, waiting for the rinse and spit and bolt from the chair, flash of the checkbook, and mad dash through the waiting room out onto the street again, safe and longing to breathe free.

The podiatrist: the podiatrist is wearing a scary white lab coat and is brandishing surgically sharp tools around your feet, cutting and trimming corns, dead flesh while you neurally cringe, waiting for the slash. He is chatty. Chatty men with sharp instruments make you nervous.

"What do you do for a living?" he asks.

"I am a writer."

"Oh boy, do I have a story for you."

You know with a dead certainty that a man who trims bunions for a living does not have a story for you. But what can you do? One is not rude to a man who is armed to the canine teeth with blades, who wears a white coat, and has a tray table arsenal beside him. So you do not sigh. You glaze your eyes while he tells an interminable story about a trick toe. And it isn't even that tricky a toe; Mr. Ed could at least talk. You long for the waiting room. You have dreams of glossy magazines about Tom Cruise's latest babe and fly fishing in Canada. Every nerve in your body is coiled to spring from the table into your shoes at a second's notice.

"So," he sums up. "You can write that one if you want it."

Like Hermes you are winging through the waiting room. You are history, golden, gone.

The train: the woman who glommed onto you in the waiting room—late train—has just dropped onto the seat beside you. Silently you protest. There is no God. "So," she asks, "what do you do for a living?"

You think of groaning. You think of lying. Tell her you're an exorcist. Tell her you're a back-alley abortionist. That will shut her up. But, no, she'd say, What an interesting line of work. How many demons a day? Or, Do you guys still use coat hangers? Nothing would be too awful for this woman to imagine. A woman who carries a plastic flamingo purse knows no shame.

"I am a writer."

"Do I ever have a story for you."

You are resigned. You are a Gandhi-ji of conversational long suffering. You are the Mother Theresa, the patron saint of platitudinous mercy. You settle back for a long listen. You watch the landscape rolling. You converse with your watch. Something about her aunt and a gallbladder operation. You are not a nice person. You are profound in your misery. But your mama brought you up right, so you nod and mumble, Interesting, which it is decidedly not, imagining the train platform onto which you will leap for your life to merge anonymously into the crowd. Free at last. Thank God Almighty. Free at last.

Love: here, your smart-alecky inner voice deserts you. You cannot be glib. You cannot be facetious. There is nothing funny about love thwarted. Nothing. You write in the second person to abstract yourself from the pain of waiting, waiting for love to happen. Waiting for a phone to ring. Your name inked in his hand on a creamy envelope in your mailbox. Waiting for a ring for that empty finger. But second person does not abstract you from the pain. It's a convention, a literary device. There is always a second person.

Eight years ago I fell in love for the first time and the last time in my life. I fell gloriously. I fell completely. I fell disastrously in love. A parachutist without a rip cord. A fallen woman. A massive oak tree crashing, thudding, making a sound, making the ground quake with fear. These are metaphors. They are not sexual metaphors. They do not begin to approximate the extent of the fall, its seriousness. Wile E. Coyote never fell from a precipice more vertiginous. Charlie Chaplin never executed a more artistic stumble. I know why they call it falling, falling in love. It's working without a net.

I have nightmares about falling. They land me reflexively in bed and awake. But I do not have a fear of falling so much as a fear of landing. It's the impact, after all, that hurts. Crash-landing. And that is where I found myself in love. Crash-landed with a man who could not love me, or could not continue to love me, or could not love me well enough. I am still trying to figure it out. I am still waiting. Time, I have plenty of, overmuch of. Plenty of time to think. Idle hands. The devil's playthings.

After eight years, I still wait because I cannot stop loving him. There is no understudy, no surrogate who will do. There is he. And there is a world of not-he's. The talk show goddesses say,

Snap out of it. But it's not a trance although it is a state of being. Waiting. Life is what happens while we wait for something else to happen. Waiting is my form of life, of love. And if he did not exist, I would have to invent him, because waiting is preferable to the alternative. No expectation. A mouthful of latex fingers tasting like disgust. The truth: your heart is full of ashes and dried rose petals. He no longer even thinks of you. You are slimmer than a memory, paler than a ghost of a wisp of a chance. Waiting is a way to subvert hard truth. The last recourse of a jackass. I am an expert at it. Practice makes perfect. It's a solemn business, waiting.

Ohio: I moved to Ohio for a job. I am convinced that that is the only reason anyone would ever move to Ohio. No one ever stops by in Ohio. The only reason to go there is because you have no other choice. No one ever passes through. No one ever goes there by accident. It is the ultimate waiting room. Everyone is waiting to get out.

I presume too much of course. I admit I am a chauvinistic New Englander. But I do not lack conviction: there is nothing to do in Ohio and there is way too much time to do it in. The food is bad, the climate intolerable, the landscape grim. I have been waiting to get out of Ohio since I arrived here. If I could claw my way out of here, I would. I have never disposed of my moving cartons. They are waiting more patiently than I, stacked neatly in my garage, ready to move on the moment.

All the imagination in the world cannot convert Ohio into a metaphor for something acceptable, and God knows I've tried. I have tried to raise in my imagination the hills into mountains, the snake-infested, murky, sluggish waters into freshet-freshened mountain lakes. I have tried to convert their iceberg and cling peach salads into radicchio and endive. For a year, I struggled mightily. I made some progress. But six years have a way of eroding even a confirmed dreamer's confections. Like meringues, the metaphors fell, leaving me with the undisguised unglamorous reality that is Ohio.

There is a reason that Ohio is in the Midwest. They stuck it there because no one wants it cluttering up the pretty places. Sure, if you've never lived in a pretty place and cannot imagine breathable air, good taste, food, and disposable income, you would think it was paradise. But breathing in the summer is like trying to inhale a sponge. Food is what you stuff into yourself to keep that orange complexion and paunch. Clothes are opportunities to masquerade as a billboard in slogan caps and T-shirts.

I live in the worst of it. The old mining corner where Kentucky, West Virginia, and Ohio commit incest. All of the towns are sad. All of the towns look the same. The buildings rotting into the ground. The birds listless. Dusty sleepy towns whose old Victorians hum some half-remembered tune of a long-dead hopeful future. Abandoned mines. Indian burial grounds. Homes sinking dismally into the clay and poverty. Neglected graveyards. People came here mainly to die. The hills are sinuous with mysterious folds and hollows and secrets and suspicious hilljacks. One marks seasons by their shades of grayness. The sunlessness, the gray ground. The winter offers no snow to soften the blow, or just stingy storms. It is habitable for two weeks a year, one in October, one in May. It is a place one could only love when leaving it.

And it has a sinister seductive beauty. And some day, after I have left here, I will write stories about this place. But not now, not yet. I am too claustrophobically here, as alien to this landscape as it is to me. I am too much at argument with it. It is the only place in which I have ever lived that I have hated, passionately, vehemently hated. I resent it too much to write about it. I cannot bear to think about Ohio. Hatred. It is not an emotion that sits comfortably with me.

Ohio. So he could not live here; hence I wait. And how could I fault him for not wanting to live here? I don't want to live here.

And so I wait, my heart full of him as a way to bear these gray days in Ohio. My bitchiness is my therapy. It is all that stands, as flimsy a construct as it is, between me and despair, between me and futility. I will not give in to Ohio. I am indomitable, a descendant of Old Yankee Stock, people lunatic enough to build stubborn homes on hillsides that get blasted several months a year, strafed by winds whetted to a fine blade by temperatures unknown in Ohio, by snowstorms unthinkable in Ohio. And I miss them. I miss them terribly. I miss them like I miss him.

Ohio is my sensory deprivation tank, my penance, my purgatory. The waiting room for heaven, which is anywhere but here. And, truth, if I have not been kind to Ohio, it has been kind to me. My son has thrived here. My first real job, here. My first writing award, here. My first book, published while here. But the price of this? The forfeiture? Love. Home. It is too dear.

But here in Ohio a man told me his story, hoping that I would tell it for him. It is a story about waiting. A perfect Ohio story. He did have a story to tell. Stories are about a different quality of waiting.

But wait. First, a digression. People who tell you that they have a story to tell, do not. They confuse stories with anecdotes. They do not understand that, while the pleasure is in delay, delay involves selection, a sexual toying with information withheld and disclosed. A bore is a narrator who does not understand language, love, tone, or the difference between the significant and insignificant detail. A bore doesn't know love's language, its quirkiness, its mystery. A bore tells you everything.

This is an essay and not a story. Some day I may shape this same material as a story. But the essay is a recalcitrant form, a flexible form, a resistant form. It is a way to transmute self-loathing into something of beauty. For me, it is a way, too, of refining material that might eventually be subject to the constraints of fiction's different formal demands. But I can hide in fiction; I cannot hide in an essay. Essay is virtual reality, virtual not in the common and casual use of its meaning, but its exacting and exact meaning. Virtual: essential. The virtual essence. Virtual truth. In the essay, I can run but not hide. Fiction conceals me. Always first the truth of the essay, the hard light of the essay before I drop the layers of veiling fiction which yield nonetheless their own variant of truth. Syd Lea said once in a lecture that an essay must contain a grain of truth, however small. And the truth is never small.

This is old-fashioned of me, I confess, but in both forms the leap to metaphor from the individual truth to the larger encompassing one pertains. "Education by metaphor." Frost's term. In poetry, in the personal essay, in fiction: truth is truth. Words across a page. And truth knows no genre.

So the truth. In Ohio I am solitary, sometimes lonely. I long for society. I want for company. In my second year here, I hired a photographer to do a shoot for me because I needed pictures to accompany some publications. He arrived, a handsome, tall man, with a sweet face, high color, a gentle manner.

He posed me, staged me, arranged my hair, but no sparks. Okay, I thought, not his type. But I respected his work. He composed me. I loved the photographs, and we became friends. I was somehow aware of a woman he'd been dating, a statuesque redhead. But they no longer seemed to be seeing each other.

We met several times for dinner, movies, drinks. He was working exclusively freelance, and I could not understand what kept him here in this dismal little corner of Ohio.

He smoked too much. He drank recklessly at times. And the demons with which he struggled were evident in the darkness that occasionally scudded over his face, occluding his gentleness. He had an edgy bitterness whose source I could not divine. But it made me want to extend kindnesses to him, gifts, gestures of friendship, of good will. And his evident but unexpressed pain touched me.

His birthday, like my son's, fell on Saint Patrick's Day, so a few years into our friendship I offered to take him out to dinner with my son. Who was this man who entered the pretty, high-ceilinged anteroom of the restaurant, face blooming, arms full, full of a bouquet of flowers, riotous with flowers? This was a man transformed.

During dinner he drank moderately and appreciatively his Merlot. He ate with pleasure, commenting on the sauces. His smiles were irrepressible, infectious. They made me forget Ohio. He charmed. He twinkled—forget and forgive the cliché—he twinkled. He really did.

It was one of those perfect dinners that are memorable even as they happen—the company right, the laughs heartfelt, the food, its perfection or disappointment unnoticed because the mood is so right and spring is beginning and the universe seems possible again.

At some point he leaned over and said, "I need to show you something. Once your son is gone."

I nodded. Heck, yes, there must be an explanation for this Ovidian metamorphosis. If he told me that he had just learned that he was a dryad released, I would not have been surprised. Eventually my son went out to explore the adjacent playground and my photographer friend went out to his car.

When he returned he dropped a creased, crumpled, timeworn yellow slip onto the table. It was a lab report. It was dated the year of my son's birth. It had his name on the top. It was an HIV test. A ballpoint-blue X marked the positive box. Oh, dear.

I still wasn't getting it. I studied his face. He shook his head. "I have another lab slip," he said. "I got it this week. No. Negative."

Then I understood—still only partially.

One fact can click all the component information into place like the keystone brick that holds the wall together. This one fact. Now I understood the recklessness. If one is dying, why not smoke, drink too much? Why not hole up in Ohio waiting to die? Why not black moods? Despair?

A month later in the car, he handed me the other missing jigsaw piece. He was gay. Therefore the relationship with the girlfriend, which could never happen. Therefore its failure. We came to love each other, came to love each other enough that he felt free enough to say to me once that, if I were hung like a Hemingway bull, he'd love me in another sense, and we could both laugh. Strangely enough, now we had sparks. Sparks of love and understanding and trust. Enough trust that he gave me this story to write.

It has a happy non-ending. He had some delicious frivolous affairs. He no longer gave away his belongings because he was preparing to die; he gave them away because he was preparing to move. He moved to Santa Fe, then Colorado, changed course and careers, left the dark, waiting years behind. And me. He left me behind, too. But he left a large lesson with me.

We are all waiting to die. What matters is what we do with the time. It's only a question of where the finish line is drawn. And that is unknowable. I respect my friend for his years of hermitage, his moral decision of not exposing others to his disease, albeit specious disease. But if ever there was an argument for getting the second opinion—this is it. I love him for not regretting the decade-plus he lost. He viewed it simply as time regained, and that testifies highly to his indomitable spirit. But it is also a cautionary tale. It makes every second tick more loudly. I take this from it, from him; even when doom insists on his prerogatives, live your life fully and well and sensorially and completely and happily. Choose joy.

I love him for not thinking those were wasted years. But it makes me want to burrow into the transitory second, to love Ohio and my eventual release from it. It could happen. Eleven years, twenty. It could happen. Why suspend happiness? Even waiting, he taught me, can be a form of elation. Eventually. But, hell, why wait for eventually.

Living consciously, fully consciously in time is about release. I miss him, but I thrill to his new horizons, sense of possibility, his peripatetic pursuit of happiness against the consciousness of time. We best time with our hearts and consciousness. His was a double-edged story and realization, and I hand it to you as the gift it was and is to me.

Consciousness itself is so highly unlikely (and problematic). Problems first—I suspect that we are the only species which knows that it is mortal. I recall a moment in *The Right Stuff* in which an astronaut explains the difference between the courage of a monkey and an astronaut—a monkey doesn't know that he might die. That is courage of consciousness. And its gift. It makes heroes of us all. It challenges us all to live each second of life as metaphorically larger than life, larger than a latexed finger passively endured.

Passivity is the writer's pitfall. Life first, then writing. Writing allows us to transmute anything, everything, the unendurable, the durable, even what we passively endure, into the consciousness of writing. That is why my friend handed me his story. That is why I am writing this, to find in his story its meaning, its consciousness.

Being fully conscious is about release, yes, but also about embrace. Unconsciousness becomes unthinkable then. Becomes unthinkable now. Now.

Now, nothing can make me flinch. Not the failed love. Not waiting. Because even waiting delivers. Delivers a story about waiting, which delivers me from myself. A life on whom nothing is wasted. The examined life. A life fully lived. Writing is my life fully lived.

And Ohio? These profound gifts. That story. That friendship. Even that dentist and podiatrist and the gallbladder lady. See? It's all here. Like many writers in exile, I learned from my alien place to discover my place. Ohio gave me this gift; unlike many Americans at least I know where home is. And I will die trying to claw my way with my un-latexed fingers back there. Home. It's a concept and a place. And I can get there even on the late train. Or die trying. Trying. That's enough. Life may be a waiting room, but it's worth the wait. Consider the alternative.

Forsaken Places

I have long loved abandoned places. It is difficult to say why. I suspect that it is their mood, the tone they evince once the people leave the landscape. Deprived of their meaning, their utility, they reveal characters, attitudes that human activity obscures.

When I was a girl my father taught for a while at R.P.I. in Troy, New York, a sad, homely, little city. For a while his office tenanted a story of an abandoned Catholic convent, sharing the floor with some ROTC officers. But the rest of the building remained undisturbed. When he took me with him into work, he let me have the run of the place. We rode up to his floor in a rickety old cage elevator with a chipped, red-and-white tile floor. Then he left me to explore on dusty afternoons the derelict classrooms, the nuns' empty cells, the chapel.

The building smelled of limy crumbling plaster, varnish, and evaporated holy water, something ropy but faint, a hint of sacred incense? The walls were painted that faded penitential green favored by institutions in the fifties and sixties, a non-color intended as a form of penance or corporal punishment. The nuns' cells were the saddest rooms, small, low-ceilinged, Spartan, murmuring of bruised knees, forgotten longings, missionary moonlight streaming in from the external world through judas peep windows on sleepless nights. Fonts still hung on the walls inside the doors, rimmed by stain lines from evaporated holy water.

In the chapel, the red vinyl on the prie-dieux crackled, a gash of white cotton tuft foaming like spittle from the red, dried lips. A plastic grimace. But soft-colored lights sifted onto the unswept floor, the stacked pews from the stained glass window above the chancel.

The classrooms were cruel. Wooden desks uninscribed with the initials of puppy love looked sternly forward, the anonymous seats polished by the dutiful standing, sitting, standing, no slouching ever, of what bodies, what daydreaming students who had graduated to what futures, where. Uncracked transoms over the doors. A frieze of a rigidly ruled, cursive alphabet, upper and lower case, underlining the ceiling moldings. The diminishing echoes of an oak ruler across knuckles followed by no outcries, a catechism of small humiliations learned by rote.

The center courtyard choked on a garden of neglect. The weeds ran riot. A stunted apple tree hunched miserably in a corner over a lichened stone bench. The sole gesture toward prettiness in this place that time cowed into a deepening asceticism of desuetude.

What about this place spoke to me? It is difficult to articulate a mood because, as we name it, it eludes us. But I found peace there in its whispers of sacrifice and suppressed feminine lives, in its ghostly round of duties, its transitoriness perhaps. Its bricked ephemery. A place that had outlived its usefulness, its vocation.

Happy places are too bright for me, too clamorous to touch me in that place that is mood rather than emotion, that ineffable quiet chapel where we all abide, mysterious to ourselves and others. Give me the bandstand in Central Park in Schenectady, New York, after the last brass note has blared, after the applause has ended, the tubas have all been packed away, and an unseen bagpiper haunts the air with a plaintive ballad on a mournful rainy afternoon in October as slick leaves litter the ground. Give me York Beach after the last tired, sunburned vacationer has packed the car with sandy beach chairs, after the taffy shops are boarded up, the pennants furled, the amusement park rides stilled, where the waves do what waves do when no one is there to ride the breakers, where the beaches stretch with their detritus leaving only the seagulls to pick through the shells and gnarls of seaweed and salt-bleached cans. November. A kiteless sky. A hermit crab pokes tentatively from a shell. Only my footsteps mar the hard band of wet sand. Am I perhaps in love with my loneliness?

But it is larger than loneliness alone. The semantics of subject and object. Place as the site of perception.

What does the summerhouse do while I am gone? A mouse nests in a pillow that I neglected to put into mothballs. A spider tats undisturbed in a corner of the window through which I am not staring at my ring of mountains. As snow sifts over the sills, mounds to the windows, the cobweb flutters, ragged. The spider is gone. An ice jam leaks quietly during the January thaw into the corner eave of my bedroom.

After I have tinned the candles and the soaps, stripped the beds, stored the linens, packed up my clothing and meanings, what does this place mean, how does it mean? Does place have an immanent meaning when my arrival is not imminent? Does my house brood?

Dust settles and shifts. Time passes. I, revenant, open the windows, shake out the linens, sweep up the dust, banish the cobwebs, restore meanings. Do I dust aside some abiding meaning of this place? Does its meaning shift?

In February the frozen heartwood of a maple cracks in my absence. A tree falls in the forest. In my shredded pillow, a mouse curls more tightly in sleep. What does a mouse dream? Are its dreams small or large?

Going from here to there in the seventies my parents used to roll through Sharon Springs, past the rotting Renaissance Revival grandeur of the Roseboro Hotel, closed in 1968. The tragedy of the loss of its former beauty gave way to another haunted beauty. A strange, secondary beauty. A history of taffeta rustles in the ballroom. The demure swish swish of lacy fans before cool faces. The creak of empty rockers on its verandah. The spectral sounds of people at pleasure and leisure in a slower time. Pace. Time speeds up as there is less of it to enjoy. I could not bear to see the Roseboro restored today. I will not return to Sharon Springs. I am nearing fifty. I will not live to see the Renaissance Revival of the Renaissance Revival hotel. I could not live with it. I doubt that I will see my own revival. A person does not have the immanent meaning of place. No inherence. Is that why I write this essay? The hotel rises again, but the mineral springs dried up long ago. That meaning bubbled away.

Would someone please ask the maître d'hôtel, who dances in the ballroom now? Would someone please ask the concierge if the young girls still wear pearls? There are no names on my dance card. I leave pink lipstick stains on my pillow at night; they are more indelible than I. Perhaps that is why I like the quiet wildness of abandoned places. I am a missed opportunity. I want to haunt some future place, leave some susurrating sheen of fabric, some soft click of pearls.

I find these desolate places more civilized than the places I am forced to inhabit as I age. I sympathize with their decrepitude, with the stately decorum of time. Places that have outlived their usefulness observe time's poetry, the forward march of iambic feet. Spanning time, they scan it. I similarly scan for meaning, survey these places. Iamb. A heartbeat. It's over in a heartbeat. I am. Still I am. I am still.

Their stillness appeals to me because I am similarly still while time is not. I live for the larger portion of the year in a still center in a still town which is still alien to me after seven years' residence. I must live there because my job is there. Athens, Ohio, a dusty, sleepy town in a southeastern corner of the Midwest, a town that shows the strain of the westward movement, what is left behind when people push through—Victorian houses peely with blistered paint. Like grand dames tarted up and fading in brothels past their prime. It is a college town that strains for meaning when the students leave on vacation taking with them their hormonal happiness, their bottled glee, and untidy notebooks, their pouchy knapsacks. Then the past settles into the streets like nostalgic pollen. No traffic disturbs it. The restaurants close. The windows blink darkly. The buildings huddle on acute hills. On Court Street, orchestral chords from a long ago demolished hotel filter into the December dusk while a withered whiskery man collects cans from the curb in the half-light, stooping for them from a rusty bicycle, tossing them into a wire basket mounted on the rickety rear fender. It is a scene that only Hopper could paint.

I love Hopper for his omniscience about the mood of place. How his settings absorb the people in them, their angularity, and abstractedness into landscape. They are architectural. Postures. Only the hard edge of light, of time, of place pertains. That is how I feel in Athens, Ohio. Incidental. I am still living in the summer home where a mouse dreams and the winter wind rattles the door and tatters a cobweb. In Ohio I am what a mouse dreams. The overlooked crumbs pecked at behind the cupboard.

I do not locate myself in love, but in place I find my place. That place for me is the summerhouse in Vermont, buried deep in snow now where my clock no longer ticks. Does it wait for my hand to wind it?

Time tenants these untenanted places, and that is what attracts me as a writer to haunt these haunts. The archeological dig into sunken stories. I raise, from cellar holes, houses, and unremarked families, the quiet stories, furtive glances, unexpressed hopes of unmarked lives. I remark them, mark mine among them. Setting is the formal aspect that gives stories their moods. From their settings, I uncover my own moods. I like to think that when I am no longer marking time, that time will mark me, that the settings that have moved me with their moods, moved me enough to want to rescue them from the archives of silence and vicissitudes of time by writing about them, will preserve their moods for some future reader-brooder like myself.

My favorite spot in Athens, Ohio, is the abandoned Lunatic Asylum. A glum, grim, brick Victorian building, turreted and towered, it glowers down from its ridge on the sluggish river curving around the dirty little city. Its windows are blank with the misery of its long-banished inhabitants. The doors closed in the nineteen-eighties. The windows are barred with lacy grillwork and a filigreed iron portico juts over its immense oaken double doors. It is the saddest place I have ever been, and I am content there.

I walk the cemetery with its two blasted, blighted trees posted like sentinels at its gate. A circle of numbered stones disrupts the otherwise orderly rows of similarly numbered stones. No names. No epitaphs. No dates of births and deaths. Just numbers. The dumping ground for the forgotten and unwanted. No one puts flowers on these graves. It is haunted. Haunted by ghosts half-mad with their loneliness.

I have seen old photographs of the asylum when it aspired to be a happy, hopeful place. A pet alligator on a leash in the courtyard fountain. Women in bustled dresses and elaborate hats carrying parasols. The dining room dense with velvet draperies and plants, bundles of peacock feathers in urns, lush with plants and tricked out with ornate bric-a-brac and brass gas fixtures. It has the feel of a period resort, a playground for the genteel.

But I hear different echoes when I walk the halls today: the sizzled screams of electric shock patients, mute female cries rough-handled by the night staff, closeted terrors. I stare at the stone windowsills and wonder what patient, trembling fingers carved these messages in stone, chiseled out day after day through a barely cracked window their desperation to leave something behind in this cavernous hulk of a building? And why are all the Ns in the inscriptions reversed? What do they encode? One of the inscriptions on the window ledge refers me to Romans: 3, the N again reversed. I read: they are all gone out of the way, they are together become unprofitable: there is none that doeth good, no, not one. Their throat *is* an open sepulchre; with their tongues they have used deceit; the poison of asps *is* under their lips.

Is this the scripture of the benighted? Is it a prayer for deliverance?

Behind some of the steel doors I read cryptic messages scratched in the paint or scrawled with what? Blood? Ash? Excrement? "I did not get tricked saying it so I didn't do it." "I only wanted a cigarette." These small stories scratched into these sprawling walls. How tiny are some lives. How large are they all. It would be sweet to redeem them, to scoop them all up like some impossible bouquet of daffodils and gladioli, of yellow roses and daisies, and heaps of forget-me-not, to plunk them into some huge crystal vase and never let the stems get soggy, the water murky. How pretty to pretend. How pretty to pretend that you bear some riotous bouquet into this solemn building and present them to all these lost and forgotten numbered people, and say, "Here take these. Take them all." I have remembered you. Tell me your names.

I recall a scene in the movie biography of Lenny Bruce. He sent his stripper girlfriend a room of flowers, flowers run amok, a funhouse of flowers, a universe of flowers that looked so crazy, so full that only a deity or nature could invent that much profusion, send that many blossoms and blooms and sprigs and sprays. How the girlfriend laughed. That fullness. That is what it means to feel life, to feel love. As I watched that scene, I thought, yes, that is what I want—that over-muchness that draws up the full-throated laughter of delight. I did want that. But I didn't understand that it was a metaphor for something else, something other. I wanted, just once, to feel fully there, fully in love as if love were a place, an instant in a place that brims over because it is perfect—a girl in a gingham dress sitting on a rock who blooms beautifully in her lover's eyes. A walk alone along a rainy street by a bridge when no one sees you, but you carry someone in your heart until your heart knows no edges. The first glance, startled but unsurprised. You? So you are here at last. Why did you arrive so late at the dance? I've been waiting . . .

These are the moments of abandon I sense in abandoned places. Moments of abandon obscured by the solemn mood of their abandonment. I stand in their quiet rooms waiting for someone to speak to me. Perhaps it is my own voice I long to hear in these quiet rooms. What are you feeling, I ask myself. Or perhaps I am waiting for some stranger to speak and ease the strangeness. To make me know surely and fully what I am feeling. Is that life, finally, tiptoeing through some desolate room waiting for a stranger to speak? Where are you? I've been waiting. Speak to me now. I am in the ballroom in my prettiest dress and waiting to hear your voice. Let's leave something of ourselves, our love behind in this aging world. Speak to me now. Now.

Raising Abel

Three years ago I hiked with my son up Okemo Mountain to the fire tower on the summit. It is a slender skeletal tower which sways with the wind like a top-heavy daisy, and it commands the broadest view of the mountains in our section of Vermont. As a girl, I climbed it with my father to breathe the fulgent, slightly humic tang of October and to locate our hill, florid with maples, and the little star-shaped lake in our town, Belmont.

In my teens and twenties, I climbed the tower with my brother and a group of friends, and we sat in our aerie drinking wine and smoking and talking. Rocking in our cradle beneath a silver rocker of a moon and a starlight-netted sky, I understood what a hawk feels, riding the currents. The air there is sharper, cleaner than logic; it clears the head. I wanted my son to breathe it.

As my son and I bumped and tripped over the rocky end of the trail, nearing the tower, I could hear voices, curses, whiff reefer, the sulfuric imminence of violence. Uh oh. But this was my mountain, too. My tower. I glanced at my son. We were going up.

We reached the tower base. Splintered and splattered over the granite outcropping, great splashes of red. Glass. Blood?

No, triangular shards of glass gouged from the red splotches. Jars. Jars of spaghetti sauce. The hooting voices floated down. Bottom feeders. Another jar whistled to the rock. Smack. Red sauce splattered the leg of my jeans. Glass strafed the boulder. I grabbed my son's hand. Stupidity coupled with enthusiasm was a dangerous combination. I knew carp who were smarter than that crew in the tower.

Imagine carp. Now imagine carp being riled up by a Great White motivational speaker. Now toss in some dope. Imagine stoned carp. Riled-up stoned carp. That's stupidity with teeth. Staring into the maws of idiocy was not the reason I'd climbed the mountain. But the image haunts me, troubles me still. It is an image of the culture that we have become and one from which I desperately want to protect my son.

What bothers me? The gratuitousness of the violence, the inanity of the activity. The creativity of the destructiveness. I mean *who* over the age of two is going to find dropping bottled foodstuffs and watching them go splat a form of entertainment? And the total disregard for the beauty of the setting and others' right to enjoy it. An almost unspeakably imbecilic disrespect for place and other people. Oh, yes, and the disregard for my son's safety. *We could put a kid's eye out. Splat. Heh heh. Rock my world.* And my intuition that this scene could escalate quickly into some sort of Brothers Deliverance violation, that I and my son were unsafe in this world, yes, that infuriated me. And it nettles me most that I know that today the world is more theirs than mine. Lord of the Flea-brains. Splat. Heh heh.

Now picture that brain trust four years from now, CEOs, government officials, teachers . . . Splat. I am beginning to understand our foreign policy.

I am living in Vermont this year on my sabbatical. Generally I spend only summers here, and I hate leaving at the end of the summer when crickets chirp, blackberry season is fading, meteor showers sprinkle the night skies, and the cold edge of fall sneaks into the air and tiptoes across the frosty fields, rustling the cornstalks. I hate leaving when the light turns blue and the air has the crisp clarity of crunching into a Macintosh apple. I inhabit weather, and it, me. The clarity affects my imagination. I think better in the fall. I hate to leave when we are entering my favorite time of year to return to the sodden steam bath of Ohio. This year I am staying on in Vermont and watching with personal interest the housekeeping excitement of the chipmunks on my doorstep, gathering in their seed stores. I know exactly how they feel. I'll be here, too.

Last night was the first cold night that I have spent here in seven years, one worthy of a fire in the woodstove. I opened the firebox door and startled. A dead meadowlark lay neatly on the bed of ash. I cried. Somehow I imagined what it must be like to fly into a chimney pipe, beat your way to an exit, only to find yourself chambered with cold ash, your heart and wings beating uselessly as you slowly starve, slowly thirst, in a darkness smelling of damp ash. Suffocating. If only I had been in the house when the bird flew into the chimney. Surely, it raised a fuss, clattered, clanged in the pipe, the stove. But in a summerhouse in the fall, no one is there to hear a bird trapped in a stovepipe, no one is there to rise, to cross the braided rug, to prop the screen door open, to lift the latch on the stove, and free a frightened lark who will fly out to its meadowed world and join its own, an exultation of larks.

I know what that feels like, to find myself—heart beating like wings—in the wrong place. I feel it more and more frequently these days. I had no sense of how long the bird had been dead. I could not bear to look at it too closely. I built my fire and burned it where it lay. It seemed the only decent elegy, to send its spirit up with the smoke, up the chimney that it had flown down.

Lark's pyre. Small bird makes small smoke. I plant larkspur in my garden.

In Ohio we have a chain-link fence in the backyard. I spotted some shape in its corner a year ago. I saw two crows conferring, stepping forward with shrewd caution. *Is it food yet?* A rabbit had tried to wriggle through one of the diamonds in the link and gotten stuck. The original dumb bunny. No going forward, no going back. It had died there. Again, had I noticed it just an hour earlier, perhaps, perhaps . . .

I paid my son ten dollars to remove it to the woods. I gave him leather gloves to handle the bunny and told him to wave the crows off. Crows are cruel pragmatists. They have a scavenger's eye for opportunity. Raucous. Cacophony. *Is it safe yet, do you think, to peck out its eyes?* Crow caucus.

My son earned his money. I could not bear the imagined feel of the rabbit's sinewy body in the leather palms of the gloves. Rabbit in fence. Me in Ohio. Stuck. How do I get back home, to Vermont, or even near Vermont?

I had a trailer hitch put on my car so that I could tow a year's worth of belongings to Vermont. I was en route to pick up my trailer when the truck ahead of me struck a deer. Traffic stopped. Blood everywhere. The deer lay crippled, directly in front of my car. The truck pulled onto the shoulder. Deer's eyes rolled white. Pain and terror. It bleated. The men approached. So terrified was the deer that it kept trying to rise, to run, to flee on its broken legs; it would hump up onto its twisted legs only to collapse onto its breast, smashing into the tarmac. Over and over again. The men tried to wrestle the deer to the side of the road. I could not watch its animal panic, its animal suffering. I covered my face with my hands. I realized that I was yelling in the way that one dimly realizes that one is dreaming when a dream becomes too unbearable and some merciful consciousness cuts in, emends it, reassures our sleeping self, It is only a dream. No, I yelled. No. No. No. Help him. Help him.

The man's bloodied hands were on my windshield. *Ma'am. Ma'am. Are you okay?* I think that I told him then about the veterinarian just down at the corner. I know that I drove away as soon as I could pass. I know that over and over again the scene thudded behind my eyes like the yearling's breast crashing into the pavement. I called the game warden when I got home. I called him back for several days. He consoled me that they had splinted the yearling's legs. I believe that he lied to me. I know the cure for horses who limp. It makes a loud report.

Later the road was clear. Truck gone. Deer gone. Only a wide, brick-colored stain, the width of a lane. So we mark our passing.

What do these scenes have in common? What do they tell me about myself? I do not handle the pain of others well; it becomes my own. That, too, I do not handle well. I do not handle death, its wantonness, well. I do not handle destructiveness well. (Splat. Is it food yet?) This may be compassion. It may also be its lack. And I may be too much in love with beauty, with prettiness. But I can tell you that the horror is deep, genuine, animal in its reflexivity.

Perhaps my greatest objection to Ohio, my southeastern corner of it, is aesthetic. I do not find it pretty with its red clay soil, viney woods, shallow lakes, dust, gray skies, clammy climate, speed bump hills. And this section of the state has about it that Southern air of regret, a place that knows that it was once a better place, a grander place, like some spectral inbred aunt who keeps peeking out of an upstairs window from her boarded-up, sun-blistered Victorian. It is a sad place. When I am there, I am sad, too. I miss my mountains. I miss the cold. I miss snow. My temperament is blizzard. A cold that can scour you clean. Snow that squeaks underfoot with cold knowledge.

My son also loves the cold, but he is angry at me today. Today was the first day of school. In Vermont. He misses his Ohio friends. But his resentment soon eases. He says, "I know that you have earned this year. It's fair. But I hope that you have a really, really great year."

I know what he means; he is going to have a really, really miserable year. But he is making a gift of it to me. It makes me sting with love for him. I struggle to get my legs beneath me, to rise. I hug him. I am raising Abel, not Cain. And my Abel has become an Ohioan.

It is more than aesthetics, of course. For one thing, there are an inordinate number of Republicans in Ohio. Ohio Republicans are not like Vermont Republicans who are socially progressive and environmentally and fiscally conservative. Ohio Republicans tend to say things like, "Homosexuals are abominations." They invoke God and the bible. A lot. They hang flags in places where God never intended flags to be hung. I have too many conversations in Ohio that sound like spaghetti jars smashing on rocks. I have a Yankee's aversion to waste.

After school my son told me that he skipped lunch today, avoided the cafeteria. Instead he went outside during lunch period and sat under a tree and sketched. He told me that he does not mind being alone. It was not, I think, bravado. He has inherited, I fear, my solitary aspect.

Lately I have caught myself staring into the lit windows of my own house. At night I stand outside and think that the house looks as if it would be a happy place to live. But I am not certain whose frame I expect to see silhouetted between the gingham curtains, backlit by cozy yellow light. Who am I waiting for? What movement? What sudden appearance? Perhaps him? He, the one whom I still miss? Perhaps I expect to see myself, some version of myself, staring out in wonderment at the night as buttery light spills out onto the lawn. I see myself coming and going. In one Vermont folktale a man who shares my surname, Connor, meets himself down by the swamp. The moment of meeting yourself coming and going is the moment of your passing, according to that tale. I am always coming and going and meeting myself on the other side of a windowpane. Sometimes I think that I am leaking all over the universe. The scrim between what's within and what's without wears thin. I do not wish such a solitariness on my son.

I have, of course, known all along where this essay is headed, where I planned to take it. I did not wish to deceive you; I only wanted to ease you there. We are nearly there.

In the sixties my father taught at a (now defunct) small college in Maine. We rented a rambling yellow house across from the college and sometimes boarded students, one of whom, Joe, became family.

What I remember about Joe—

He was quick to laugh. His cheeks were so ruddy that they appeared polished like Cordovan shoes. He let a raccoon chase him out of the barn one night when he went to empty the garbage. He was lanky, and when he sat for us three kids, he brought over pretty girls who giggled softly and said, "Joe, no. What if Doc and Mary come home?" He helped my father to shingle the roof and paint all of the shutters black when Mom and Dad bought their own house in a neighboring town. He dated girls whose names began with J and gave them black pearls for engagement rings. He loved Jo Stafford and took his girlfriends out to dinner at steakhouses. He sold sporting equipment on the side. My dad said that he was an operator, but he laughed when he said it. He had crinkled black hair. He attended the plays that my younger brother and I wrote and starred in, staged in our dining room or barn lofts. He was a lousy student but a good basketball player. He enjoyed dressing like he thought students dressed (letter sweaters, loafers) and once startled my mom into convulsive laughter when he stilted storklike into the hall in corduroy shorts with snowflake knee socks, his long, hairy white legs stretching between hem and hem. He laughed, too, so hard that he knocked his studious glasses down the stairs. He and my dad went on fishing trips. He loved Jackie Gleason. And my dad. They traveled to Ireland together. He flunked out of college. Whenever he came to visit us, he arrived with laughter and cold on his coat and armfuls of gifts. He always smelled good; he wore Canoe. There was a series of jobs, in sales, I think. Dad was the best man at his wedding. I loved him. We all loved him. His eyes were blue and faceted with light like my mother's aquamarine pinkie ring. Delphinium blue, larkspur. He vanished.

Perhaps to bear them, we make legends of our losses. Over the years around our kitchen table, we tried to explain our loss to ourselves. He was in jail. Embezzlement. The marriage had failed. Dad wrote letters to his last known address, saying that nothing Joe could do, had done, might do, might have done, could ever compromise their friendship or the family's regard and love for him. We contacted his old college friends for news of him. We wrote his family members. We placed ads in Connecticut newspapers. Silence.

Why, we asked each other. Do you think . . . We missed him. We were baffled. Then an obituary arrived in the mail. No return address.

Thirty years had passed.

Joe died in his early sixties. My father is still in his late seventies and has bested cancer twice. I am nearing fifty. We are no longer baffled. But the explanation after so many years, so many irretrievable years, is a paltry thing.

Joe had become an elected official. He cared for his ill wife. He lost a son. He often spoke, according to his friend who contacted us after Joe's death, of a family in Maine whom he had loved and with whom he'd lost touch. The friend sent the obituary, which explained why Joe had chosen to remain lost to touch.

The obit claimed that Joe was a college graduate. Not only did it claim that he had graduated, but it also claimed that he had graduated from a university that he had never attended, let alone flunked out of. There it was. The public man could not bear the exposure, the shame.

But my father claims that he knew even that, that Joe had told him once on the phone that he'd falsely claimed on a job application that he had a college degree. My father claims that he even told Joe to forget about it, that on the scale of human sins it was niggling.

But I believe that was why Joe fell out of touch. For three decades. Thirty years. Half his life. The waste of it appalls me. Joe? Dead, you know.

When my son was five, we moved from DC to Connecticut. First snow, first winter, we rolled Norman's first snowman in front of our Cape before he caught the bus. Norman dressed him in his own clothing, even included mittens so that his twig hands would not get cold, and, always a divergent thinker, Norman gave his little man antlers.

While he was in school, I worked in my study. The sun burned off the yellow-gray clouds of the morning and glittered through the bubbled glass in the windowpanes. When I went out to meet Norman, the antlered man (rein-man?) was just a damp heap of sticks and clothes.

Norman was angry and heartbroken, demanded to know where the snowman had gone. I tried to explain, but he would not believe me because any explanation was preferable—that I'd hidden him, that someone had stolen him, that he'd walked to the ice cream shop—to the truth: that he was gone, simply gone. The untenable evanescence of memory, of life. Of love? That too?

We, volant, fly into dark cylinders, chambered with our terror. We lurch on broken legs. We ensnare ourselves in our fences. And all, all that is forgivable if accidental. But to will it? That is the smack and splatter of spaghetti jars.

What do I want now from Joe, from my son? I want my son to know that no vanity is worth mistrusting love. I want Joe to know that I spend hours trembling on the verge of sleep in vertiginous empathy: what must it be like to outlive one's own son? I can imagine no greater pain. How foolish we appear before the relentless eye of sun. Snowmen, we roll ourselves tall, trickle to this: a soggy heap, a stain on the pavement, then nothing. We need love for this: to mark each other's passing.

My father recently told me a story about climbing to the fire tower in the fifties. It had been a season of no rain. Late spring. The ranger up there was muttering mad. *Let them find their own fires, by God. I'm up to here, staring at hills, trees, trees, and more trees. Not a drop of rain. I'm telling you, first drop, I'm out of here and I am not ever coming back, no sir, and if they think otherwise, they got another think coming. Hell, I'd almost be happy to see some smoke, burn down the whole state forest, then I could go home and stop squinting at trees, spend some time with the bride. Never mind the kids.* He ranted on, his neat tie bobbing in the collar on his pressed shirt.

The summer was hot and dry. After Labor Day, my mom and dad again climbed the mountain to watch the sunset. There at the base of the tower sat the same ranger, looking considerably more disheveled, the brown uniform a rumple, the tidy tie now askew. He scrambled to his feet with a goggle-eyed glee. "Come see. Come see," he called, motioning, "come see what I've done." He ascended the tower, taking the steps two, three at a time. "Come."

My father was wary, sensing the neural verve of someone

who'd been alone on the ward too long, but he took my mother's hand and they slowly ascended the tower. There on the floor of the upper platform amid curls of bark and pine pitch was the outcome of this ranger's long watch. He had whittled away his loneliness and tedium, carving a village, a train, a collection of whistles and figurines, and friendship spoons with volute handles, twined hearts.

This fall when I climb the tower with my son again, the jarheads and whittling ranger will be long gone. My son and I will scan for fires, wait for rain, make art of our lonely hours, and I'll send up a wisp of prayer, a thin plume of smoke. My love for Joe.

Last night I could not sleep. Quarter moon beyond my window, its orange silhouette a face in profile like an illustration in a nursery book. I smiled, its familiarity a golden glow in my window. I was inside my own house, the dark silhouette framed by my curtains looking out at the moon who peeped in. I knew that face. I know it still. It is the face of everyone whom I have ever loved, keeping watch on the watchtower, watching over these campfires we lay with cabined kindling in our hearts, burning safely out with small smoke. We watch and wait. And then the rain comes, and we go home.

The World Before Mirrors

On Christmas Eve I am in Vermont on sabbatical from my teaching job in Ohio, and I receive a call from the ghost of romance past, my college boyfriend whom I have not seen for thirty years. He has a multisyllabic name. He makes me laugh. He tells me sad stories.

One: he moves to Paris, gets married, and becomes a junkie.

Two: he moves back to New York, wanders homeless and drunk and schizophrenic the streets and shelters, in and out of Bellevue. He loses his memory.

I cry for him, and he says, "Do not be sad. I got to realize my goals. I always wanted to be a junkie in Paris, and, to a prep-school boy growing up on the Cape, Bellevue always had a gothic romantic allure. I always wanted to go there."

This is bad boho poetry. The romance of decadence. The romance of madness. And where was I while he was wandering a lunatic labyrinth of alleys? In Connecticut. A housewife.

"A Connecticut housewife? You?" he asks me. He weeps for me.

We have both lost years.

This is how Gregory Harrison Hollander found me.

In a Brooklyn bookstore stall he found a copy of a literary journal published twelve years ago. In the journal he found a story written twenty years ago under my name. In the story he found a version of his name. Via the Internet and my name and my father's name, he located me and called me on Christmas Eve. It was the most interesting gift that I received this year. More refracting than the Waterford crystal from my mother, more amusing (although less useful) than the power tool set from my father.

Today is January twelfth and it is lightly snowing, a careless sift of snow. It has snowed every day since Halloween, my first New England winter since I moved to Ohio in 1995. I am thinking about Gregory and how little I remember about him and how this is the first time that I have ever written an essay about events as they are occurring, a contemporaneous meditation. Present tense, but I think that this essay is about the past, about memory and how it forgets, about love, about loss.

What I remembered about Gregory before he called:

His eyes were blue and sparkle with a hint of I-Wouldn't-Drink-the-Kool-Aid-Around-Here.

He had the posture of a question mark.

He wore blue jeans well and denim shirts.

He had a blurting laugh, simian manners, and dressed and spoke like a man who had cowboy dreams.

That we once made love in Clarendon Gorge on a rock as polished and curvaceous as a Henry Moore sculpture.

Once after smoking too much pot we found a plastic bag of something squooshy and scary (intestinal?) in the woods and could not talk about it.

That a spooky nocturnal named Eugene lived on his dormitory floor and used to tail me at night when I scurried down the hall to use the bathroom, smashing out light bulbs in the ceiling as he followed, panting and laughing.

That he painted and had painstaking penmanship.

That he gave me a sterling-silver ring shaped like a helmet which my son covets.

How often have I thought of him over the last three decades? Not at all. Or perhaps only when I wear the silver ring, which is not often, and then I have thought of him without any detail of recollection. But why was I unwilling to give my son the ring? Because it was a gift?

Memories that I do not have but accept from Gregory now on faith:

That he and I rolled down the hill in sleeping bags, which made my father hopping mad.

That I peed in a sink in a men's room, skirt bunched around thighs, talking speed-of-light-heartedly.

That I was his first. His first first.

That we snuggled on my brother's dormitory floor in Boston.

That we first met in boarding school when I asked him to find me a chair at a movie. I was a dismissible hallucination, one among many.

That we went to an ox pull at a county fair.

That he (that you) carved our initials in a heart on a tree in a corner of my father's meadow, that you carved it with a buck knife, carved it hard, carved it deep, so that it would last, that you believe that you could still find it. And I did not have the heart to tell you that it is likely long gone, cleared to accommodate the pond that my father wanted there. But I cannot tell you how much I love knowing, how much I love remembering what I cannot remember, that once someone, you, loved me enough to carve a heart in bark, that the landscape of your memory is unaltered, that I am flattered and shaken to my leaves to know that I was ever, ever that young, and that I want suddenly and again to roll down a hill in a sleeping bag. I want that more than food and sleep and oxygen, more than coffee.

What I now remember about you that I did not before:
That your voice is gravelly, that you drawl and stammer.
That you use words that I have not heard in a long time—pest, adorable.
That you dumped me, I dimly recall, for a girl. Cathy, maybe?
That you loved a song by Wings, "Bip Bop"?

I do not remember loving you. But you told me on the phone that we loved each other. And that was why my father was so angry when we rolled down the hill in sleeping bags—because we were in love and you were fucking his daughter. I have not missed you. But now between calls I do.

Why did you enter my life now, bringing these memories with you? Memories belong to the past, are the consequence of careful editing. Next week is my birthday; I am nearing fifty. Why all this abrupt youth flittering like parti-colored litter, tattered snapshots into my aging days? Why open now this store of joy, long sealed? IT IS UNBEARABLE.

You and I agree to meet at a B and B in southern Vermont the day after my birthday. You have little money. I will pay the bill.

This time of year, erumpent night arrives before five. Dusk is my temperament. On the phone at 10 p.m. you tell me that I can tell you bedtime stories, that I can tuck you in, that you know how to rub my temples and quiet me so that I can sleep (I so rarely sleep). You tell me that if you play music to a female praying mantis and chuck her under the chin, she will not eat her mate. Droll metaphor, Gregory, but I do not pray, do not prey. We call each other several times a day. We have not seen each other in thirty years. We were a decade younger than that duration when we met. But now I can clearly see the tree, the clean incision in the bark, you laughing but just a little, at the corniness. Your cuts were precise. Time's arrow pierces Cupid's heart.

How did I forget that tree? Hearts in bark. Why have I never looked for it? I return to Vermont, to that meadow in Vermont every year.

I do not recall why we lost touch or how.

I have now lived ten years alone. I have dated, but I have not come close to falling in love, to allowing someone into my life, my home, the corners of my days when yellow sunlight spills into the room, and I find a hollow, a half-hour, an hour to read a magazine. There are reasons for my solitude: Ohio. Two failed marriages. I am raising my son alone. Men terrify me, their needing frenzy. I have habituated to my solitariness. My untenability, I have more faults than California. Too many times to the trough.

I have always thought that monogamy was a failure of imagination.

I have not had an exclusive relationship for twenty-eight years.

At the moment I have more dates than a fruitcake. I recently posted a dating site on-line. I am a first-timer. I decided that while on sabbatical I needed to take the initiative, to act, or else I would soon be posting on Geezer.com. In Ohio I spend far too much time staring out of windows. In Vermont, for some reason, I spend time in the evening standing outside my own home, staring at the snug yellow squares of light, the pretty curtains, the chandelier. I mentioned this to a friend. "Why?" he asked. "I don't know yet," I said. "I think that it is about longing."

When I pursue that thought's arc, it becomes thanatological.

I have to break frame. As I was writing just now, I startled myself. Someone in the room with me. No, I myself reflected in a black, brumal window, in Vermont, on sabbatical, working at my desk. But, yes, someone, someone else. I am wearing a sweater, pale blue, an uncharacteristic color, cashmere, a Christmas gift. The woman in the window distorts in the glass. The person, that one whom Gregory brings back to me? I owned no cashmere sweaters then. I wore Mexican wedding shirts and clunky gobs of turquoise. Now I own enough cashmere to build my own goat, enough leather to build my own cow. Visions and revisions. Versions and reversions.

I am hearing the past in my dreams, voices underwater, drowning in a flooded town. A whole town blooms and rots in the Quabbin Reservoir, Dana, Massachusetts. I am swimming in my drowned house. Am I standing outside myself when I peek into my own nighttime windows, the gothic architecture of my old, vaulted mind? Last night I dreamed that someone said to me, "You are very beautiful." Until I turned my head. Then the voice said, "My mistake. You are not beautiful at all. I did not see your nose."

Gregory, I do not see my nose.

I recall that yours was turtle-like.

In the world before mirrors, we would not have to shatter such dreams.

Particularly on Sunday afternoons in February, I feel as if I have outlived my time. In two years my son will be in college, and I suspect that I will be ready to check out of Hotel Joan. A good guest always knows when to go. (I think I'd like that for my epitaph.) This is not despair but weariness. I am tired. I've had enough. It's been a good show. I have sampled hundreds of men, loved wonderful women, driven recklessly, laughed perversely, traveled enough roads, worn jingly jewelry, danced and sung more than once until dawn, eaten well, drunk way too much, stared at skies, lived mainly in pretty places (except Ohio where I have lived the longest and which I hate with teeth-grinding clarity). I think that my work is done. I have raised my son, written my books. I have tried to love the men who chose to amble through. There is nothing sad about this feeling. My friends, I am tired. That's all.

I am especially tired of living in Ohio.

This week an editor asked me to name my favorite place in Ohio in my bio note. I wrote: the exit ramp. I lacked the temerity, however, to send it.

Ohio may be my metaphor for mortal claustrophobia.

I moved to Ohio in 1995. I now know that this was the year that Gregory got well. No longer addicted, drunk, schizophrenic. He told me on the phone that he then had to set about recovering his memory. Now he is my memory. Now he is no longer a memory. Now his memory is finer than mine. Since 1995 I have been trying to club as many brain cells as possible to death with a wine bottle. I have less and less memory and less and less need of it. There is more than one highway out of Ohio.

It occurs to me that my memory is wandering all over the country, traveling with people I know who carry these repositories of my memory with them. I have forgotten their names.

I fell in love for the last time in 1993, the way a meteorite falls, or mud slides, or hail falls. Disaster. Every time that we fall in love we alter love's quality and retroactively qualify all previous loves. The last one? I did not know that I could love anyone that much; it nullified all prior loves. Its heat scorched my past. A charwoman, I swept up the ashes of my past loves, past lives. They no longer pertained. I found myself with no edges, a huge capacity to love and asking nothing to return in kind.

I never want to feel that way again.

I no longer believe in love, or I suspect that it is overrated. Love. Shmove.

This morning Gregory wrote me about the plumb line that he tacked to his window. I recall it. It dropped next to his bed. He used it to tell time. He boiled brown rice in a corner of his room. Each memory concatenates a memory. The memories open like Chinese boxes, nested, with delicate springs and tiny hinges. I am remembering too much. I write Gregory and ask him to remember no more, tell me no more. I am living in reverse but aging forward. Frictive motion. Grinding plates.

In my sleep I grind my teeth. A man whom I did not love and with whom I slept last fall told me that I do this. Gregory told me on the phone that he has trouble sleeping with a partner. My room in Ohio faces east. I have a large pencil-post bed. Sunlight is my partner. I wake facing west.

A year ago I saw Gregory's name on a movie crawl, a credit line. I was with a date, a man as blustery as the mayor of Doodyville, so I didn't have time to give it much thought. How many Gregory Harrison Hollanders could there be? I think that I concluded that someone must have once heard the name and adopted it. A theatrical name. This happened to a former acquaintance of mine: Templeton Peck. My name is too plain for theft. But the credit line was Gregory's, my Gregory's, after all.

Gregory is my new editor, forcing me to revise my memory. I threw out his love letters a decade ago when my husband and I split our former household. I thought that I went skinny-dipping for the first time when I was forty with a girlfriend in a lake in Vermont. Stars and fireflies. We were stoned. The water felt like seal skin. I was elated to be naked under the night dome and single again.

But now I think that Gregory and I may have swum naked

together that day after making love on the rocks. In one of the troughs of the gorge. The cold water, hard nipples. Your too-blue eyes. No, I wore my panties, I think. I know why this is hurting. It is the pain of consciousness, of living in time. Our love makes such tiny ripples. I want to be young again. I want to be in love. Oh Gregory, this is such a bad idea. I am out of love and trust. IF I HAD IT TO DO OVER AGAIN, I would not.

I have earned my mistrust of men. I have been raped, beaten, strangled, pushed from a moving car, abandoned on a road at three in the morning, twenty degrees below, with no shoes and a bloody nose. My first sexual relationship was with a man in his sixties. I was three, maybe four. Memory's imprecision. I have fitted myself into so many shapes, earth mother, professional wife, tart, feeder, tender, that I could be a contortionist. Yes, I am these. But how did they NOT notice that there was someone here who preceded the masque?

I have been thinking lately that the cause of much harm in my life is the iconicism of male sexuality. What makes a lover of a child, a whore of a housewife, a waif of a woman. It is difficult to locate oneself beneath all of the visual projections. Let me be. Let me BE.

Gregory wrote me that he has incorporated the Bowman mansion into the novel on which he is working. The mansion is in Cuttingsville, Vermont, a beautiful Victorian mansion. It was a bookstore when he and I were dating. We went there once on a rainy day, so quiet that you could hear book lice munching: eat your words. A man with a disquieting high voice, penny-whistle pert, oversaw the shelves. When I turned a corner, I screamed. A woman coming at me. Wraith, I thought. I myself in a floor-to-ceiling mirror. I am what I most fear. Like the moment in the glass darkly.

Am I who I am or who I was? Are they the same? I no longer wish to be a reflection. Might I vampiric stare into an empty glass? The world before mirrors.

The mirror manifests the divided self, and Lacan theorizes that in that gap language originates. Words are how I construct my self. Without them? Knock knock. Nobody home. Ashes ashes we all fall down. Selfhood is a knock-knock joke without a punch line. Dr. Caligari's empty cupboard, Mother Hubbard.

As I write this, I am waiting for his call.

I usually try to date people I don't like. I wouldn't want to wish myself on someone I actually care for. And it isn't much fun getting naked any longer even when I am in shape and down to date weight. The skin looks like a Shar-Pei's snout. Gravity is relentless. And love is chancy.

What is the chance that Gregory would find that magazine at that moment, recognize himself and reenter my life? Is this design or coincidence? It doesn't matter. Now that it has happened, it is constative.

Recently a prep-school boyfriend attended a reading of mine. I did not recognize him until he spoke. His voice was his own. He used to be clean shaven. He wore his hair long, and he had a sleek, runner's body. Round, short-haired, he had become his opposite.

Will Gregory be foil to himself?

Similarly I recently met my former husband in a restaurant in order to pick up my son. I had not seen him in six years. I stared at the strangers, scrutinizing each until I spotted my son. The man next to my son had been my husband for fourteen years. On a street I would push by him without an inkling. My son told me that he is shopping on-line for a Philippine bride. I know what that means; I was the Philippine bride.

Life is not a dress rehearsal. This is it, kids. The real deal. Opening night.

I sit at a huge banquet table offering so many groaning pleasures. I want to taste them all. I want to eat it all. I have had difficulty with monogamy because alternate lives have always seemed possible to me. I could be a carpenter's wife in rural Vermont, or a Go-Little-Vampire-Girl in the Village. Singularity is a limitation of possibility, infinite possibility. This ensures my solitude, and the solitude protects the work.

But sometimes I think that I should just get married, married to anyone just so that I can stop dating.

What passes for love at this age may be wariness, negotiation. Perhaps we were wiser about love when we were young, ready?

A month ago I posted on an on-line dating site for the first time. A photo that my son took of me for my next book jacket and two short narratives. It took courage. In the morning I opened the site. Only ten hits, I was disappointed. Then I read them and studied the pictures—all women. Odd. Cause and effect sometimes escape me. For a while I moped about not even being able to attract a man. Then, the slow epiphanic march. I had posted as a woman seeking women.

I reposted as a woman seeking men. In the morning I opened the site. Three-thousand hits. That gave me panic attacks. I read a few. Too many Daves and Bills and Carls. Some marriage proposals. One from Germany. One from South Carolina. Some of them I suspect were automatic responses to any newly posted profile. Some lewd. Some totally full-tilt bonkers. For someone whose approach to dating over the last decade is, "Hello, I must be going," it was too much.

Some of my male friends, amused, asked to read my narratives.

They were:

Myself—I am a professor with one son about to go to college. I am currently on sabbatical in Vermont. I love to laugh, attend cultural events, cross-country ski, and work out daily. I am independent but affectionate and am looking for playmates to laugh with. After my son, my writing matters most to me. I am not seeking anything more than enrichment. Audience, company are everything. I am a kook but essentially harmless. I am quick-witted and find that this makes some men uncomfortable. The intellectually timid need not apply.

My match—No control freaks please. No axe murderers or aliens either. You like intelligent, independent women. You know who you are and are seeking enrichment, not mollycoddling or support. You have a sense of humor, love to laugh, and want to have a conversation with someone for the rest of your life. You are mature, centered, and patient and understanding, but can be spontaneous. You are as comfortable at the carnival as you are in an art museum. PLEASE no mooches. No children. I am looking for a manly man. Open-minded and open-handed.

The heading: Writer Seeks Diversion

My male friends' analysis? Of course you got a gazillion responses. Diversion means sex. Playmate means sex. You ask for no commitment. Do not mention marriage. Want no children, have a son, grown and nearly flown. Clearly work out and are fit, have your own money, go downtown and uptown. You do not mention "soul-mate," "long-term relationship," or "beaches." You are smart and witty, and the narratives are simple and direct.

Odd. And the responses? Not one conformed to the description. In the midst of this e-mail blizzard, Gregory called on Christmas Eve. I did not receive one dating inquiry from a Gregory. Not one.

Gregory called this morning. He did not call yesterday because a friend from Maine showed up in New York, took him out for steaks, bought him a stack of CDs, and corralled him into a strip club.

I tried to explain why all this remembering hurt me—as if time were a caliper and the past and present were squeezing me between their legs.

Gregory tells me that I have misremembered our break-up. Actually I precipitated it by doing something "gross." I ask him not to tell me what happened. I prefer not to remember. I know enough about myself already to cringe. I am a cosmic apology for my own existence.

Gregory owns a turtle named Monk that he found in the streets. Monk can build stairs and pyramids out of books. He can flip a heating pad onto his back. I cannot build pyramids, Monk. But memory is my carapace, the shell forming around what I need to hold onto, defining its small self by what it is infinitely excluding.

Gregory never invites anyone into his Brooklyn apartment because he only has one chair and a bed, not really even a bed. He sleeps on the floor. A friend gave him a bed, but he got rid of it. He preferred the floor. His life sounds simpler than mine.

His French girlfriend slept in a bed. The wealthy have nice beds. The French girlfriend comes with her own adjectives like a Barbie doll with her accessories—rich, artistic, French, famous. Every time that he mentions her, the same linkage of adjectives. I ask him how he recovered his memory. He demurs, defers.

Ralph Somersault was forty-two years old when he died. Gregory and I have already outlived him by several years. A nimble jester, his acrobatics landed him on his feet and in the favor of Henry VIII. He tumbled in the court and endeared himself to Anne Boleyn and she to him. But the king's love was fading. The bloom was off the rose; the head was off the queen. Poor Ralph somersaulted no more except for headlong drunken lurches into the hearth. The king dismissed him, and the besotted, sodden, untumbling fool careened from county fair to county fair cutting his dismal jigs for pennies.

I want to roll as Ralph once did but down a hill in a sleeping bag, dizzy with love, sky, grass, sky, grass, sky . . . without the sad ending.

Gregory tells me on the phone that he knows of a place where we can stay in Paris. It has no heat, and you have to haul cold water up in buckets. No, I say. No to cold water, no to sleeping on floors.

He chuckles. A nasty, right-before-I-spring-the-practical-joke chuckle. "I am presentable," he says. "I have a two-thousand-dollar suit and four-hundred-dollar shoes, a clothes horse."

Neigh, I say.

How Gregory recovered his memory, the no longer deferred story:

He had forgotten how to read. He decided that if he reread all of his own books, he would begin to recover what he had forgotten. He started teaching himself to read with some Reader's Digest condensed novel. Not only did he realize that he could read, he realized that the book that he was reading was lousy, so he started reading better books. And as he read them, he remembered them.

He then set about restoring his personal memory. He stared at his hands and tried to remember where he had gotten a particular scar, how he had broken his thumb. From his injuries he reconstructed a body of memory.

The doctors had advised against this undertaking. It worked.

I have a paper cut on my upper lip from an envelope I was licking, to seal an angry love letter. A scar on my brow where my glasses cut me later that night when I slipped, drunken, from my tub. I do not want to read any more books in that library. I keep the covers closed, the books on shelves.

Memory may be a form of repression; the blackout may be a blessing. I prefer not to remember what it hurts me to remember. I remember what I need, sometimes not even that. Memories displace each other. The teacup can only hold so much tisane.

We had a spat. I have offended Gregory. Too much of me. I don't blame him. I feel the same way about myself. He says that his mother told him never to look into a lady's handbag, and that he doesn't. He says that I am the sort who dumps the whole handbag into his lap. He is correct.

He says that I stir up passional valences. I have no idea what that means so I must write it down. I still have no idea what it means. This essay is a lady's handbag. Yes, I dump it in your lap. No, I will not apologize.

Like Monk I am building my essay in steps, but my pyramids are jerry-rigged, tilt like Caligari's set, career down Cubist corridors of time.

Gregory does not use emoticons in his e-mail; this pleases me. I find the ideogrammatic shorthand to represent emotional complexity disturbing. A smiley face, a frowny face. These do not suffice to establish tone. They are cynical representations. And what emoticon could accompany these sentences—I have five thousand dollars left. My plan had been to write until it was all gone, then kill myself.

Gregory, I do not think that I can bear that much responsibility.

The suit was a gift from the rich, French, artistic, former girlfriend.

The first emoticon was the wink, invented by Friedrich von Wink, an ambassador to King George III's court, who blinked an eye to signal a witticism or an irony. Beau Brummel derided it for its indecorousness. I simply think it facile; let the words speak for themselves.

The emoticon is the postmodernist proof of emotional impoverishment. Passional valances, window dressing.

An engram is a postulated change in neural tissue meant to explain the persistence of memory. Perhaps I cannot remember loving Gregory because I lack engrams? Can one lack a presence that is hypothetical? Yes, I suppose, because in 1993 I fell deeply in love, but the relationship was largely theoretical. He and I saw each other only once a year. And I suffered more over his inability to love me back, love me actively, not as a state of being, than I have suffered at any other time in my life. Love is like seeing quarks. The invisible, the postulate that makes the universe happen.

My memory, unlike Gregory's, lacks detail. My memories are more like impressions, ambient memories. I retain only some aura of the era. Balming air. Gardenias. Crisp shadows shivering on the lawn.

My detailed memories are not memories at all but photographs. A memory of me and Gregory on a rock outcropping. His cheeks are ruddy, and he is wearing a red shirt. I am in profile, staring at some point beyond the range of the photograph, wearing a gingham dress, blue and white. I found the photograph in my mother's album. Gregory is smiling; the smile is soft. I do not know what I am staring at or what became of that beautiful Dorothy in Oz dress.

It is fifteen degrees below this morning. On the phone Gregory asks me if he needs to bring a coat when we meet next week. When we were together, he wore a hooded red sweatshirt, sometimes with a denim jacket over it. I have emotional, temporal whiplash.

In "The Nothingness of Personality," Borges writes, "There is no whole self. It suffices to walk any distance along the inexorable rigidity that the mirrors of the past open to us in order to feel like outsiders, naively flustered by our own bygone days."

I am flustered, not naively.

If life were a line graph, a continuum of contingencies, what would it mean to reverse the line, follow time's arrow back to the instant before Gregory and I separated? Had we remained together, how would our lives have been different? His life—no France, no junk? My life—no beatings, no . . . But my son. Irreversible. Him I cannot unthink. I own my time.

The day after my forty-ninth birthday: Gregory is not foil to himself. He is as I remember him. His eyes are pellucid blue. He slouches. He is wiry and strong.

What is new? His hands and feet are tough. Less hair. His upper body cartoons itself with tattoos. Buffalo. Cat. Heart. Without his shirt, he is a bad actor, so bad an actor that he cannot disguise that he is boyish and kind. I tell him that I am not allowing my son to get piercings or tattoos until he is out of our home. Nothing irreversible. In retrospect tattoos usually seem like a bad idea.

"Oh, I've had worse," Gregory says.

How we spend time? Talking, laughing, pounding down coffee,

poking around bookstores, eating, watching a movie, sharing the Jacuzzi.

What is it like being in bed with someone after thirty years, knowing that you were his first? I do not sleep the first night. At all. I am anxious, but I cannot identify the source. I rise and read in the great room of the coach house where we are staying.

But I read and do not read. I have physical memory, my head on Gregory's chest. His body is an eighteen-year-old's body, a time machine, only parti-colored now. I return to bed.

I do not know what Gregory and I are doing. I do know that I love him. Although I have lost the capacity to fall in love anew, I have noted that I can resume loving those whom I have loved. My image of someone whom I have loved arrests with the first glimpse. He ages, but the image does not. I adjust the present to the recollection. Gregory was right; I did love him once. I love him again. But love knows many qualities.

We do not make love to each other. I do not know what that means. But we touch and kiss and talk. We are dancing lightly on some finely honed fulcrum of time. I press my head to his decorated chest. I know the attitude of his heartbeat. I know that he talks in dreams and says, "Collapsing glass takes up more space than itself." He calls out, "Mother Goose," but she does not come. Unless I am she lying still like a patch torn out of the night, curled beside this man whom I barely remember and whom I no longer need to. He is here.

I cut his ragged fingernail. I heat his coffee. I feed him mints. I pick a white hair off his black sweater.

From our bed, through the window, I see a blue bluebird house against the snow. Vivid. It is twenty below. Dawn. A melony pink suffuses the crest of the hill. How can any place that abandoned look so cheerful. Beside me, Gregory snores. He told me that he doesn't snore. He told me that pillows hurt him.

Lying beside him, I want to speak to his dreams, tell him that I love him. Is this truth or fatigue? Why am I able to imagine him coming to my home in Ohio, taking up space there, improving my conversations with the hassock? I can imagine him there, but that does not place him there, nor does it make it a good idea. Still.

We drive to our old school. It is smaller than either of us recalls. This slide from past to present to past tense makes me queasy. Carnivalesque. But we do not wear masks. For some reason when Gregory and I converse now, truth is imperative. We need to understand everything. Neither of us is coy.

On the second night, I sleep. The room's walls are lavender; I dream that I am in Provence.

I tell Gregory about meeting his father, his dog, his brothers, his stepmother. He remembers none of this. He took me to his home in Orleans and we ambled the long, sandy beaches. His father liked me. Gregory resembled him in temperament. Piney, salty, we were in love. I have a photo of him on the beach in an album in my home back in Ohio. On sabbatical in Vermont, I remember the photo, reconstruct it.

More scenes release in me. Is love a trigger, a spring unlatching? I offer memories to Gregory in nested boxes nestled in the open palms of my hands. I know from the crease over his left brow that he struggles with this remembering also. We are both inhabiting pasts that are alienating and familiar. Gregory says, "Now I have to rethink my understanding of the past fifty years. I made a mistake."

I made several. Half a century of them. Almost. Gregory has a year and a half on me.

Gregory asks me to write his memoir. "Think about it, Joan," he says. "You know how at the nuclear plants there are always two guys. We could be the two guys. Two guys with keys and guns just so that one guy can't knock down a door and take over the world. Right? Right, Joan? You and me. The guys in hazard suits, writing my memoir."

"Let me think about it," I say.

"I see," he says. "You are going to be the stable, sensible one in this collaboration."

If I am the stable, sensible one, we are doomed.

And yet and yet. Writing someone else's memoir has a certain postmodernist appeal, and Gregory's story is partly mine also. I make cameo appearances. I am the first woman to whom he makes love, the woman whom he rediscovers thirty years later, the scene arranged by an invisible hand, as Gregory maintains. I could write myself large in his memoir, larger than his screen credit, larger than the mountains in Mexico where he ran drugs, larger than the Parisian junkie wife. I could redeem him. I could make myself pertain. I could be a heroine as I never could be in my own memoir.

The past is paludal, marshy, ferny, overgrown. What have we both forgotten? I do not know about futures. Gregory has a tattoo on his arm which he can use to divine, but he did not bring a deck of cards with him to the inn. The present is very clear. We are eating frittatas in the Meadowlark Inn. Gregory will leave in an hour.

Before he leaves, he says, "You are a problem." "You are a challenge," he emends. "You are an opportunity," he concludes. An emotional declension. The way that memory moves, slides like a blue shadow over snow, slides like a plumb line dividing time on a dazzling cold white crust.

I stand on the train tracks. I cry. Strafing wind.

I do not know how to end this essay. I cannot find the exit ramp. Could it reach a degree of contemporaneity that I would find myself writing about the instant of writing about the instant of writing? Merge. Merge. All endings are leave-takings perhaps. Not a disruption but a discontinuity. Temporary. Today the wind is speaking in tongues and raises a corresponding whirlwind in me. I am trying to find the stillness inside it. The trees rattle. Weather copes with itself. Somewhere in Manhattan Gregory flaps down a street in a brown canvas coat and a black skullcap in the danse vivante not macabre. He is going to meet a friend to attend a reading. He is meeting a friend to eat his words. He carries my memories. He carries a recent memory of me—perhaps in my white coat approaching the train station, perhaps in my S.W.A.T. cap chatting up the bookstore manager about Tiny Tim? In Manhattan, he perambulates on encouraging shoes. Here in Vermont far from him I try to write myself out of time into the world before mirrors. Tenderness may be lying sleepless inside the words of another's waking dream. Collapsing glass. Gregory nudges a dog's muzzle on a ridged sand dune in 1973. The entire world is possible. Nothing is withheld. Nothing is contingent.

Blue bluebird house in snow. Untenanted. Bluebird. Blue house. Bluebird . . .

Bone Key

Every individual has an internal vocabulary of images that is permanent, completely formed by the age of 20, and that cannot be changed. The whole artistic process is the recovery of a lost world.

—JOHN MCGAHERN, *New York Times*, May 1, 2003

What is the shape of memory? The measure of loss? Does the past always play in a minor key? Lugubrious basso profundo, the sound of coral reefs miles beneath the holiday ocean's glimmer and glamour, chatoyant, ludic in the tropical sun.

I am on Key West with a lover from thirty years ago. I wanted a vacation from the hip-deep winter in Vermont, so I brought him with me. Why? For company? To measure the distance to the irrecoverable, the unrememberable, to measure the fastness of the past's grasp?

He is reading Tennessee Williams's biography beneath a poolside umbrella, the skin of his stomach as white as a potato's tuberous eyes. I lie in full sun in a white bikini, browning, freckling.

He says, "Two pages and he's already slept with six guys."

I smile. I do not say that pages are not durations of time, that time and narratives are both unmeasurable, anfractuous. Except. Except. Narratives end. Time was invented to give narratives shape. Memory shape. Perhaps to give shape to itself.

The man who accompanies me is named Geggry. That is not his real name. He called me on Christmas Eve after a thirty-year lapse. We have been speaking daily since, seen each other three times, over four months. How many pages equal four months? In that number of pages we have not slept together. We are about something other than passion. Perhaps the shape of memory, which is like a dry footprint on a marble floor. There and not. I wear a silver ring, helmet-shaped, that he gave me thirty years ago. I wore it then; I wear it now. An object slipped between ontic frames of time. An object, an action eternally happening.

Geggry says, "He had three men while his partner was in the hospital."

Tennessee Williams lived on Duncan Street in Key West. He moved the house from Bahama Street. The past here forms like reefs, like the reef that is this island, layers of the living and layers of the dead. Or like the Key West Lighthouse which was sixty-six feet high until 1894 when twenty feet were added. Underwater or into sky, it is still accretion. Like Geggry and me. There was then. Then nothing. Then now. We are trying to understand what has happened to each other in the intervening years. Maybe. Perhaps he is not trying to understand.

Geggry slaps his book onto the table and says that he wants to walk to Juliet's for coffee. He likes his coffee hot with steamed milk, covered.

I say, Fine.

We walk down to the southernmost point and turn onto Whitehead Street. My feet blistered and infected, his socked into winter shoes, black, round-toed. Cop shoes. We walk side by side. Almost. I can't keep pace, sore feet.

His forehead is sunburned, crusty and flaky. His eyes are very blue and sometimes when he looks at me they glitter like my memory of them the first time that we made love. He was a virgin. He looked very pleased.

Key West is a place where one could die of pleasure. Rum drinks, sun bounty, leisure food, a sly sexiness. Key West. Where the Calusa Indians went when there was no more south to go. Cayo Hueso. Bone Key. Bone Isle. Key West. An osteal declension.

Memory is slow music played in the Key of Bone.

Geggry's torso is a map of the past, tattoos from the New Orleans years, sunburning, only on the shoulders, skin curling up like tattered lace from his parti-colored party years, but his underbelly still white. Tattoos of buffaloes and of his murdered cat in various attitudes—looking out a window, slinking stealthily, curled dozily. His girlfriend murdered the cat.

"Why?" I asked.

"She was a slut," he said as if there were some relationship between cruelty and erotism. Perhaps he is right.

We are at Juliet's on Southard Street. There is trouble. There is always trouble somewhere. But right now it is here. Some agents are arresting the owners, something about licensing. But Geggry manages to get his cup of coffee first, the last cup that they will be selling for a while, so he is happy. While he gets his café con leche, I read the digital screen on the register. "Ham and cheese, chicken croquettes, your best bet is Juliet's. Like Romeo his Juliet, Like a flame and Crepes Suzette, your best bet's still Juliet's."

Back on the street he asks me, "What do you want to do now?"

I want him to kiss my neck. I want him to rub his stomach against my back and wrap his arms around my shoulders. I want him to tell me that I am beautiful, that he loves me, that he wants us to be together. But I don't want these things; I want him to want them. "I don't know. What do you want to do?" I ask.

Geggry says, "I am never going back to Mexico."

"Why not?"

"I don't drink anymore. You have to drink a lot to go to Mexico."

The sun combs my shoulders with sharp teeth. Burn on burn. I open my parasol.

"This is way better than Mexico," Geggry says.

I twirl the songbirds on my parasol, bright yellow and blue, and say nothing. There is a tear in the paper that allows a jag of light to rip its shadow on the sidewalk. Whitehead Street. Hemingway Street, the boulevard of lazy cats and errant roosters. Superstitions. If a cock crows after dark and his feet are cold, bad news is imminent. If a woman peeps through a keyhole on Saint Valentine's Day and sees a cock and hen, she will be married within the year. How much vision does a keyhole permit?

A keyhole vision: Geggry and I are not lock and key. We do not fit. But we walk in lockstep, lockstep and Key West, headed back to our motel, the Santa Maria where decades ago Tennessee Williams got clobbered in the bar. Now *he* could go to Mexico. He could live there forever. Hemingway, too. They were drunk enough to go to Troy, New York.

Geggry slurps at his coffee. He asks me if I remember the day that he carved our initials in a heart of bark on a birch in Vermont.

"Ou son les neiges d'an-tan?" I say.

"Huh?"

"Where are the snows of yesteryear?" I translate.

He shakes his head and scowls. I am too precious. But that is how memory disappears, a snowflake on a fingertip, melting, evaporating. Are we defined by the memories that we remember or the ones that we forget?

We are standing in front of a shop, Key West FantaSea, some kind of wedding and costume shop, to judge by the window, brides standing, fluffy and white, like meringues among snarling one-eyed pirates. *Yar.* A group of dispirited Goth kids stands outside. With the Goth trend over, where else would they go? The clubs are closed, so they congregate outside costume stores, haunting the sidewalks, their inky lips pouting, their socketed eyes lusterless, their drowned complexions, ashy and sincere in their gloom as they scuff the toes of their Doc Martens and lace-up boots on the concrete. Their black sackcloths suffocate their bodies, miserable in the tropical glare.

I am thinking about snow, about a snow in early May thirty years ago in Vermont. A sugar snow. "Do you remember that night that we built the bonfire in a snowstorm?" I ask him.

"Look at that," he says. He is pointing at a basket of skulls mounted on poles outside the costume shop. They grin gleefully, woodenly at the Goth-goyles. "I got to get one of those."

He is not going to answer my question, the skulls a tergiversation piece.

We dodge a couple of scooters and cross the street so that Geggry can pick out a skull. They are imported from Mexico, Dia de Los Muertos, happy to be dead sober and out of Mexico.

Inside the store is cool and two well-dressed clerks go over receipts and inventory lists, murmuring. Geggry picks through the skeleton heads and skull masks and pirate costumes while I look at the Victorian wedding corsets and the dainty bridal wreaths, woven of dried tea roses and baby's breath. I try on a peasant blouse figured with Jolly Rogers.

Geggry grins. "You look pretty enough for a jolly rogering," he says.

I do not know how to respond. Is he flirting? Joking? But I buy the blouse. Geggry buys the skull.

On the street the Goth kids are still mustering their gloom. Geggry walks ahead of me.

"Stop," I say, and he turns around.

"Look," I say. "What exactly are we doing here? We start seeing each other again after a thirty-year lapse. What is this? What are we doing?"

"What," he says and he squints at me.

I twist the silver helmet ring and ask, "Do you love me?"

He laughs. "You're funny," he says. "You're more fun than things that are not fun."

I don't laugh.

A cloud of blue butterflies wafts by him, a flutter cluster. "Did you know that butterflies mate by bumping heads?" he asks. He waves his skull scepter.

"Just once, Geggry, why don't you surprise me? Why don't you answer a direct question?"

"I will surprise you slowly," he says and he smiles, one of those slow smiles that people who like the adjective *enigmatic* practice.

It makes me want to throw a tire iron at him. I keep walking on my blister-sore feet, but I try out a gait that screams SULLEN, UNHAPPY, FED UP TO HERE.

As we pass the Hemingway house a little bearded cat peers out through the gate. His round green eyes follow me solemnly. He nods. Definitely sullen, he agrees with his eyes. But it's wasted on Geggry who is ignoring me, brandishing his skull, slugging his coffee merrily. And why wouldn't he be merry? I paid his fare, his room and board for a week's vacation in Key West. He has no money. It was that or come alone. This is not a place to be alone, the sunburned revelers, the horny schoolboys, the seasoned locals with their chocolate tans, and bleached-out mullet tails hanging down their backs, their tattoos, and baggy jams. The schoolboys want pussy parietals. The locals want fatter wallets. It's a dangerous world.

Geggry has finished his coffee and wants to step into a deli for bottled water. While I pay the clerk, I say, "Who would think that butterflies mate by butting heads. It feels so retro, like those Goth kids. Punk butterflies. Headbangers."

The clerk stares at me. Geggry sneers. "It was a joke, dummy." I've been played. "Jokes are usually funny," I say and accept the change from the clerk. Small coin.

I don't mind the small con, but I feel cheated. How much larger with possibility the world was a minute ago when butterflies mated like delicate wrestlers.

Our room in the Santa Maria is shuttered and close. Geggry is napping. He naps a lot. He has turned off the air conditioner. It is too dark to read. I can't watch television, so I lie on my bed and watch Geggry, wrapped in a chrysalis of his bed sheets. He talks in his sleep, murmurs hypnagogically.

I think about bonfires in the snow. Geggry was wearing a red shirt. When the pine branches caught, they launched a spume of sparks into the snowy night sky. Two elemental storms swirling into each other, spark to flake. Flame to ice. Some of the snowflakes hissed as they extinguished in the sift of snow. Geggry and I danced around the fire, and I slid my hands under his red shirt and felt his back muscles slide beneath my palms, pulling him hard to my chest.

His chest now tattooed. A decorated memory. No longer mine. Three decades between. Sometimes when we walk, he holds my hand and it is a strange hand and familiar, both at once. His touch thirty years ago? A snowflake dowsed in a spark. All dark.

Geggry's foot twitches while he sleeps. We have *I Love Lucy* beds—he, his; I, mine. What did I expect? Did I hope for something, something corny and romantic, breezes rustling the palm fronds, Geggry and me lying on the beach lazily stroking each other, telling stories in low voices, sultry and secretive as the shadows of cats?

If time is a construct and memory obtains to the past, perhaps hope and anticipation are future memory without any facts to go on. And what is dreaming? Future memory, too? And past?

Geggry is dreaming out loud again. He says, "Suppurating eyes." I think that's what he says.

"What?" I ask softly.

Then he blinks, instantly awake, Ginny doll eyes. "Oh, hi, Joan," he says. "I was just dreaming about you." He sits up and hugs himself, bounces his calves up and down on the mattress as if he is feeling cute. He yawns and moans, a comedy of mannerisms. "So what you been doing?"

"Watching you sleep."

"Man," he says. "You got it bad."

I wonder what *it* is. "Actually, there wasn't much else to do. What are suppurating eyes?"

"Huh?"

"You said it in your sleep."

"Oh that. I had some weird form of malaria in Mexico. My eyes pussed while I read *Maldoror* in a shower stall, trying to cool off."

"When was that?"

"So," he says through a yawn, "do you think that the hand of fate brought us together again?"

"The hand of fate? The hand of Geggry. You called me, remember?"

"Oh, yeah. Right." He links his fingers and stretches long and high. The tattoos on his chest elongate, Silly Putty cartoons. He swings out of bed. I hope that he will stop and kiss me, but he shambles to the sink and splashes water on his face. "I want to go check out the cemetery," he says. He sounds like a man drowning.

The cemetery is vaulted because scant soil lies on the coral limestone. Roosters scurry between the monuments. Geggry squints in the sun. He scribbles in his notebook as he reads the epitaphs. He says that he is working on a novel. I wander along one of the sun-pounded paths. According to a story I read, Elena Hoyos, a Cuban beauty, was once entombed here. Her tomb exploded when Count Carl von Cosel disappeared from Key West.

Count von Cosel was neither, neither Count nor von Cosel. He was Carl Tanzler, who left a family behind in Zephyr Hills, Florida, and moved into a house on Flagler Avenue in the 1930s. He claimed to be an X-ray technician and he worked in the local hospital where he met Elena, in the advanced stages of tuberculosis. He was decades older than she.

Back in Germany Tanzler had had a dream about his future bride, veiled, a dark-haired, dark-eyed apparition with full pouty lips. Elena fulfilled the dream, lifted the veil, and the count began an ardent courtship of her. But Elena soon died.

The count had her embalmed and entombed in a crypt that had a telephone so that we could continue to speak with his deceased beloved. He then exhumed her. Despite embalmment, her body had decomposed, so the count set about restoring her with wax and plaster, glass eyes, locks of hair. Silk replaced her rotted skin. He put a ring on her finger, a white satin dress on her body, and installed her in the wedding bed. Time and death would make no cuckold of him. He would have his way. He knew her as his wife. He played tunes for her upon the pump organ in their small chamber.

After his arrest, the case went untried. The count returned to Zephyr Hills, and a few hours after his departure, Elena's tomb exploded.

I see the count, balding, bearded, gaunt, hunched over the organ keys, his bespectacled eyes peering at the sheet music, as he played postcoital love songs on the wheezy organ for his glass-eyed bride. While she was a trifle unresponsive, in other respects she was consummate — complacent, attentive, quiet. The perfect wife.

A grim story but a love story nonetheless. Tanzel suffered perhaps from a surfeit of imagination. Megalomaniacal, he believed that he could bring her back from the dead. Is this what became of those who could not relinquish the past?

When Geggry approaches me, I am leaning against the chain-link fence and crying.

He cuffs my shoulder, "Hey, what's wrong?"

But I cannot explain. I do not remember much of my past with him. And what I do remember? I do not want it back that badly. I would not become a countess, a grave robber. I never want to go back. But I miss some quality from that time. Innocence?

Geggry pulls me into his shoulder. He smells like himself. He smells like the past. I look beyond his shoulder and watch the hens scurry among the tombs. I feel like a paper shadow ripped with light.

We eat dinner at Coco Bistro. I pay the bill. I pay all the bills. Geggry and I met in prep school thirty years ago. We dated for a year of college. Then he dropped out, out of school, out of my life. I followed a conventional route. I went to graduate school. Twice. I married. Twice. I divorced. Twice. I became a professor, a writer.

Geggry became a junkie, a drunk, a street person, lived in Mexico, New Orleans, Texas, Paris, New York, L.A., Bellevue. He worked in the circus, led tours in the Yucatan, wrote book blurbs for a university press, did custom metal work, odd-jobbed for the movies. Each city had a girlfriend. Several. Sober now for almost a decade, he is destitute. But he tends to land on cat's feet.

Time is a sheet of collapsing glass taking up more space than itself. A line from his dreams.

Geggry told me about an episode that I cannot recall, the last time that we saw each other thirty years ago. I had been dating someone else, was single again. He said that I was "gross." I asked him not to recount it; I could not bear any more of my own ugliness. He told me anyway. I was slumming for lust in all the right places, making out with tractor trash, said that I wanted to be the Emily Dickinson of tractor trash. My armpits were bushy. When he told me, I cringed. Now I must remember it. But there might be a danger in accepting his version; it might be wrong. That decade is lost to me. Geggry brings me back time unrevised. But he could be wrong; surely, he could be wrong. *The tractor held but just ourselves verisimilarly.*

We stroll back along Duval Street. I stumble a little, pleasantly drunk. Roosters and hens rustle the bushes. I recognize the little, bearded cat from Whitehead Street on the sidewalk ahead. He looks like a little, furry white ghost. He has that cat way about him, of containing himself, being still, as if he thinks that he is invisible.

"Look." I point.

"What?"

But the cat is gone.

Geggry shakes his head. "Psycho triller, qu'est-ce que c'est?"

But it *was* there; just now it's gone.

In the motel room, Geggry is watching TV with Skully. A rerun of a *Survivors* episode. He tells the skull how he got his name; he could not pronounce "r" as a child.

Apparently not an "o" either.

Gregory. Geggry. A word game, like the game of Ghosts.

When I was a girl we played Ghosts in the Graveyard, a tag game. When you are young, it is possible to think that nostalgia is ornamental. As you age you begin to understand that it is profound. It is how the world outgrows us as our memories fix us in the flex of space, of time.

"This isn't going to work out? Is it?" I ask.

The survivors squat by the campfire. Geggry squints at me, shakes his head at Skully. "Don't be such a gloomy Gus."

Gus was a ghost. He was merry. A book I read as a child.

"You were nicer when you were younger," I say.

Geggry throws his arm around Skully on the bed and peers myopically through his unframed narrow lenses at the TV. "That's because I didn't know anything." He cackles at the private joke.

"You were way nicer," I say.

"You weren't," he says.

The TV is loud; he is going deaf. "Do you want to go to the beach?" I ask.

"It's night," he says.

I go alone.

The water is calm at South Beach, the tower of the Victorian mansion spiraling into a sky champagne-fizzy with stars. Tennessee Williams loved this beach. I understand. The wind is soft. The tide is low. I have to wade far to swim. I think how I am sharing the water with sea horses, crabs, the rusting remnant rail of the Overseas Railway, the living and the dead. Unseen. Like me here swimming at midnight. I feel fragile and transparent in my sea horse skin.

Henry Flagler, oil baron, inspired lunatic, undertook construction of a railroad from Miami to Cuba. He reached Key West. Dogged visionary fueled by a surfeit of imagination and money with no regard to the cost in time, in lives, in labor, ten years, 700 lives, fifty million dollars, his first train arrived in 1912.

In 1935 the Overseas Railroad disappeared in a seventeen-foot tidal surge. A cable fouled the engine of the hurricane rescue train. Six hundred bodies were recovered. The unrecovered were uncounted. The rails lie deep where no trains run.

The salt water stings my blistered feet. I want a hurricane to whirl into my memory, disconnect Miami from Key West, derail time, me and Geggry. As I breaststroke beyond the breakwater, stars blizzard around me like snowflakes in a firestorm.

The count learned that there is no future in the past. He and Henry Flagler are the divided self that is Key West, Janus-headed, one looking forward, the other looking back. A doomed mating like me and Geggry, just butterflies bumping heads.

Prokofiev said of the ballet, *Romeo and Juliet,* "Dead people can't dance." *To avoid love and its regret, Your best bet is Juliet's.*

I stroke back to shore, invisible as a cat, which is perhaps the object of all longing, invisibility. Life is the damage that experience does to consciousness.

I towel off on the beach. The sand grits, grinding at my foot sores.

I no longer want Geggry to kiss me, a fortunate resolution since he does not want to. What I want is to kiss Geggry again for the first time. A butterfly flicker of time. A butterfly kiss, eyelashes against a cheek. The impossibility is a blessing. We have known enough damage. I, too, was nicer when I was younger. I wrap the towel around my waist and snug it tight as if it could hold me together, enclose this internal universe of hurt and misplaced longing. This Janus-headed abomination of consciousness. Forgive me my desire to be loved. It is unbearable, as unbearable as being loved. Love is the delusion of children without memories. A song in the key of bone. It plays out.

The count constructed a wingless airship. I understand why. To be with his bride, untethered, by the constraints of gravity, time, convention.

Prolepsis. There is nothing left but to walk back to the motel where Geggry will be asleep in a stuffy room, a skull calaca keeping vigil. In consciousness I will beg silent forgiveness for the ugliness of desire from an unconscious god, as indifferent as a hurricane. The TV will still be on, lambent chatter, electronic prayer. I will snap it off. A year from now I will find some memento from this trip, a postcard, a pirate shirt, and I will find my own desire, my past desire, strange as if someone else had taken this trip with Geggry, sent me a postcard, Wish you were here. What *was* I thinking? I will wonder. Memento mori.

As I walk back to the motel, the bearded cat will spook out of the shadows on the street, open its mouth and say, "There is no more south to go."

And I will head there.

Masque

In Rutland, Vermont, I am sitting in a Mexican bar with three lesbian crows who are drinking, yes, shots of Cuervo Gold. Behind us at the café tables bounce eight enthusiastic Japanese acrobats in black and white kimonos who apparently speak no English. In walk nine Gilligans with their sailor caps pulled down to their eyes, their white ducks and deck shoes nautically neat, clapping each other on their red-sweatered shoulders and calling each other "little buddy." A woman in leopard-skin pants who is either obtuse or drunk or both is trying to scream a knowledge of English into the acrobats. "We are happy that you are here." "WE ARE SO GLAD TO HAVE YOU IN OUR CITY." Volume and meaning are all one to her, this even though an interpreter is carefully translating for the leopard lady to the genial Japanese who nod and grin and bounce. The lesbian crows are cawing it up raucously at the bar and spanking down their shot glasses. The Gilligans are ordering mai tais. Only the interpreter knows what the Japanese are ordering, but they are humming along in high spirits with the Gilligans to a snatch of the theme song, "the skipper, too, the millionaire and his wife, the movie star, the professor and Mary Ann . . ."

This is less odd than it might sound. It is Halloween. What *is* perhaps odd is that I am entirely comfortable here, elated, even ecstatic and would be even if it were not Halloween. Let me put it this way—if there were a town named Reality, I'd live slightly to the west of it. Not *in* Loonyland but certainly within commuting distance, definitely in the suburbs, and with a turbocharged SUV. I haven't lived in a viable zip code since 1967. This may explain why I have so much trouble getting a date.

Recently I tried an on-line date. He lived out of town—about two hours away. We'd met a few times for café mocha, for samosas, for bruschetta. A steamy UN ragout of dates, a smorgasbord of rendezvous. In order to expedite our romance, I invited him to stay overnight for the weekend, granted, separate beds and rooms, and no sampling, ethnic or otherwise.

It got off to a shaky start. My sixteen-year-old son, Norman, came home after school and a track meet, and my on-liner, Carlo, confided that kids made him wiggy. I suggested that we go for a hike. We were halfway up the mountain when a cloud busted over our heads like a halved hot tub. It is difficult to look alluring when one's clothing and hair are plastered to one as skeletally taut as a Chihuahua's bristled pelt. We soggily slogged back to my place where, toweled down, Carlo dealt with his discomfiture around my son by playing guitar and singing interminable, interchangeable folk songs in a Neil Young Nancy boy voice. I went to bed.

When he went to bed, I got up. The music had finally reached the end of its diminuendo like the fade-out on an old forty-five. And I have chronic insomnia, so I tiptoed down the stairs and chugged a couple of goblets of claret. As I was tipsily tiptoeing back to bed, I heard a hiss.

"Sss. Sss. Mom. Mom, it's important." Norman's face loomed white in his midnight room.

"What?"

Norman punched a pillow into his lap and whispered, "I don't trust that guy. He looks too normal."

"Maybe he is normal."

"Mom, don't be naive. All serial killers look normal. That's how they get away with it."

"You think he's a serial killer?"

"Look at him."

He had a point. He did look normal.

"He is going to kill us in the night." The pillowcase rustled.

When I have slugged down the better part of a bottle of wine, a sudden lucidity settles on me that, when I have not slugged down the better part of a bottle of wine, I would be more inclined to call *delusion* or *paranoia*. But claret-ed up, I knew that Norman was right. What we had on our hands, in our house, in our guest bedroom was a topnotch psychotic folk-singing serial killer who went wiggy around sixteen-year-old boys. I did the only rational thing that one could do after such a realization; I tiptoed back down to the kitchen and armed myself to the teeth. I tiptoed back to Norman's room, "clinking and clanking and clattering like a collection of caliginous junk," and armed him also. We sat on the edge of his bed with bread knives poised to accompany Hitchcock's EE-EE-EE soundtrack.

Despite the mother in the attic, Norman fell asleep and the knives thunked to the floor.

The wine, however, was only just hitting its mark, and pointedly, like a sideshow knife-thrower. With vinous lucidity, which has, in my extensive experience, a cumulative effect, a snowball-rolling-down-a-hill-deluding-itself-that-it-gathers-no-snow-or -reckless-speed-as-it-tumbles-ass-over-tea-kettle sort-of effect, I decided that one in the morning was precisely the appropriate time to call the two references that Carlo had given me—his ex-wife and a job contact. At one in the morning I realized with terrifying perspicacity that he had given me their names and numbers ONLY because he knew that, in so doing, I would never double-check, that it was a tactic in his psycho-sexual-socio-pathological strategy, that the women and their numbers did not exist, but that he counted on, he COMPLETELY counted on my gullibility and trust and susceptibility NOT to call, and that there was nothing else for me to do at (now) one thirty in the morning except to tiptoe down the stairs and make the two calls with a butter knife clenched in my fist and a serrated knife in my teeth, which my nearly worn-off red lipstick was giving a slightly feral cast to in light of the hour and the lightness of the bottle.

I fumbled for the phone and dialed the numbers. The first one rang. No answer. Hmm. Suspicious. Who, in this era, does not have an answering machine or service? I dialed the second number. Also no answer. Neural alarms triggered up and down my spine, my arms, my fingers. Sweet Jesus. I was piecing it all together. His odd response while in conversation earlier that afternoon when I had revealed a painful memory. (He had smiled.) Lizzie Borden's stepbrother was sleeping in my guest room.

I tiptoed back upstairs and tapped Norman. He mumbled sleepily. "What? What?"

I whispered, "Norman, wake up. Something isn't right."

He bumped up. "What, Mom? What?"

"I think that you were right about that guy. I think that he might be dangerous."

Norman tightened. "What? Why?"

"It's just this afternoon when we were talking I told Carlo about something that had hurt me very much, and when I looked up at him, he was grinning."

"What? What hurt you?"

"That isn't important. It was just his response that was weird."

It was important, but too important to tell Norman. I had been telling Carlo that someone had molested me for years, and when I glanced up, he had a twisted smile on his face, lemon peel and a stubbed cigarette in an empty highball glass. I watched him consciously readjust his face to appear solemn, appropriate. But it gave me the willies. Like watching a mask slip. A mask slip on a mask and on another mask . . . I shivered and pulled a blanket around Norman and me, crooked my knees and tucked in my feet. And there we sat, eyes glittery with fear in the gloom of the room, blades flashing in the shaft of moonlight.

Meanwhile in a parallel universe:

Carlo awakes to a susurrus of whispers. Below stairs, something clinks. Footsteps up the stairs and down. Sparks up his spine and down. More clunking. What did he really know about this woman? And her son for that matter, all that hair and those wild eyes. Gawd. What was she rattling at two in the morning? Maybe she was schizo. Maybe he was schizo. Maybe they were a schizo mother-son team who lured men to the guest bedroom then sliced them up and buried them in the daffodil beds. And she'd tried to lead him up the mountain in a thunderstorm. She really was trying to kill him. And that sexual abuse? Maybe that was a lie. The son was doing the mother and they had to kill potential suitors to protect their kinky secret and Mommy dearest. Oh GAWD. What had he blundered into?

He reached for the floor and felt for his pants. Stealth, silence. He mustn't make a sound. He zipped his jeans as quietly as he could, stuffed his feet into his boots, and buttoned his shirt.

Remain calm. He drew some deep breaths and tried to slow his heart.

Okay: here was the plan. He would stand quietly, muster himself, then bolt for the door, hit the stairs, make a dash for his car, and he was out of there, golden. He wasn't about to become daffodil mulch.

He stood. He gathered himself. He made his move.

Of course we heard Carlo preparing to burst out of the bedroom. Trembling and terrified, we rose, well-armed with kitchen cutlery and stumbled into the hall, flicked on the light as he exploded out the door. He yowled. We shrieked. This went on for a while.

The relationship didn't work out.

Love eludes me. Like the Tin Man I need an oilcan. If I only had a heart, but Professor Marvel, I don't suppose that there is anything in that little black bag for me. My future holds laptop dances but no lap dances, alas. So Carlo fled. Who was that masked man? I wanted to thank him. And here I sit again, the lone ranger ranging in the forested heart of my desire on Halloween in a bar, getting well-oiled with the lesbian crows. The one on my right has pushed back her beak to down another shot, so that her crow self is staring at the ceiling, and her woman self is staring pie-eyed at me.

My earliest recollected terror was a mask. I was two and my father came home wearing an Indian mask. When he spoke through the slotted mouth, my father's voice resonated, and I screamed. Really screamed. And kept screaming when he removed it.

What did I think then, my earlier self? That my father, my known and beloved father, was not himself or that the Indian had eaten him? Was some reality concept violated? Persona, a speaking through. The Indian mask was ruddy, with high cheekbones, lips in a grimace, and three startling, rigid feathers protruded from the top. It still visits me in nightmares.

When Carlo, calmer after the dueling banshees episode, prepared to leave, I apologized. I said that I'd call, that I'd like to take him out to lunch sometime. He said, "You are already out to lunch." He had a point. As he escaped, I prayed that his references did not have caller ID. Morning dawns with a clarity of a different cast, not colored by claret.

Once I wore a mask at Mardi Gras, a harlequin mask with a heart and a halved face, red and white, with teardrop, spiky-mascara eyes. In the mask, I became strange to myself. I flitted like a girly-girl and flirted with men on the street. I pushed aside a woman who peered at me too closely. I was not myself. The anonymity of the mask was liberating and terrifying. Invasion of the body snatchers. Who was this woman who is not I and is I? This halved stranger with her fairy-tale-colored face?

The mask is some interstitital presence that mediates between me and all that is other. The stranger who walks between us. The mask is the shape which contains me and gives identity a form.

The part of me beneath the mask who was I and not the mask recoiled from the other masks around me—the cats, and feathered fantasies, the lizard heads, and popped eyes, the leering weirdness of it. That people are not who they are is frightening, because I know that it is deeply, primevally true. The swish of costumes, the rustle of concealed identities, the aggressive disguise with the revealed eyes still peering knowingly, tauntingly through, Guess who? The sinister seductiveness of it. Carnival, the danse macabre. That tap on your shoulder asking you to dance? Yes, that may be death's brumal hand. It has a familiar and a practiced touch.

Identity is constructed and reality, too. And my hold on both is tenuous. But I like spectrally passing back and forth between realms, through ontological veils. Is this why I write? To pass back and forth? To construct an I on both sides of the Great Divide?

When I took my son on vacation to Venice, I felt as if we were floating on painted streets. The light shimmering on the water and the facades, too beautiful to bear, made me blink. And Venice surprised me in another way; an inordinate number of extremely well-groomed crazy people strode about in enthusiastic conversations with themselves or their imaginary friends. When I remarked on the sartorial splendor and apparent well-being of Venetian schizophrenics, Norman squinted at me.

"Mom." He took my shoulders and adjusted my coat collar, the hang of my shoulder bag. "They are talking on phones, cell phones, earphones. See the wires?"

Ah, the wonders of miniaturization. Norman's reality adjustment disappointed me a little bit, however. It was pleasant if only for a while to think that Venice teemed with nattily attired, histrionic schizophrenics in leather and cashmere coats and silk ties, handsomely knotted, and snazzy haircuts, and strutted the streets of this visionary city in their chic sleek shoes. It was good for my heart to think that their society could and would care so well for them. I could use such care. I need a keeper. Care.

I try not to care, but I do. In the adrenaline decompression session after the little knife incident, Carlo kindly confided that he'd been on anti-depressants and that he had taken a sedative after our hike, so that the incident really might have been much worse. He was a bubbling stew of chemicals. A Club Med unto himself. After he got off his parting shot about "out to lunch," after his car lurched out of my driveway, I got off one of my own. Too late for his ringing ears. The esprit d'escalier. "So my prince finally came; too bad he was Prince Valium." The belated moment of nastiness did not improve my disposition, not one whit.

The medieval masque is an allegory, so, what, you might ask, does Carlo stand for? Apparently not for knife brandishing. He couldn't stand me. I took it sitting down. He said that I was too alpha female for him. Alpha? Little did he know. In love, I'm Alfalfa, maybe, a little rascal. But Alpha? I am Omega, the comedienne of the pack. The low, lower, lowest slapstickler of love. The pratfall from grace. My alpha wave: bye-bye.

The lesbian crow with the beaky wizard's cap clearly has a bead on me. The other two, fondly fondling each other, are obviously a couple. But this stray crow smickers at me, eyes louche. I don't mind; I'm flattered. Sexuality, too, is a mask which we posit between this gender attraction or that. A great fluctuating tidal amorphous longing that, like water, takes on the shape of its container. I am a fem man at heart. I bat my eyes like batwings at her, and she falls off her stool.

Crossing over. Desire has no contours. But I've always thought that full-blown bisexuality would be exhausting. In Venice I would have had lubricious whiplash. All those beautiful men and women. Head spinning like a cock weathervane — Hey, that looks good. Whoops, yum. Over there at three o'clock. Yikes, heading this way, heading this way and talking to herself. *Oh Mama if I only had my youth.* A cornucopia of concupiscence.

Nope, that would spin me like Dorothy's house. Crash-landing.

I am well-mentored in masks from a young age. Pedophiles are masters of the masquerade. Mine taught me well how to read expressions, that lecherous meanness that sparks lizardly in the eye as a man says one thing and means another. I learned to hear the hollows of words, their shadow selves. "Would you like to go get a root beer?" meant "I am going to hurt you." I learned that gestures and touches have barbs that dig deep into flesh. I learned to read faces and words and touches for their ulterior alterities.

I learned the game of eyes. I learned how to use language and wit to avoid this man. And when he cornered me, I learned how to abstract myself from myself, make a mask of myself so that I could regard through the mask's slotted eyes all of this happening to someone who was not I. My pedophile, in short, made me a writer. But I will decline to thank him for the education.

When I was in Venice, as sensorially delighted as I was, linguistically I was catatonic. I am accustomed to being able to articulate even subtle and complicated and refined thoughts and moods and responses. Language is my arsenal and refuge. Banter is my form of flirtation. Tongueless, I am selfless. I feel profoundly isolated when I travel where I do not know the language. To sense but not to be able to express: an aphasia of the imagination. To connect but not to be able to communicate: an autism of emotion. I could, I suppose, run screaming through the streets like the leopard-skinned lady, trying to will the universe into understanding me with belligerent decibels. But I know that noise and meaning do not equate.

My next foreign trip will be to France, and I do not speak French, so I have been reading the Lonely Planet French phrasebook. Naturally I immediately leap to "Dating & Romance," and it is discouraging.

Si on buvait quelque chose?
Tu est de quel signe?
Je crois que je tombe amoureux.
Quel est ton numéro de téléphone?
Tu veux venir chez moi?
Tu veux entrer un instant?
Embrasse-moi. Allons au lit. Attache-moi.

J'aimerais partir maintenant.
Ne me touchez pas!

Laissez-moi tranquille.

Je ne vous trouve pas attirant.

On doit refaire.

Mais NON. See how quickly it can all go wrong. It is indeed a lonely planet. A few phrases, a page or less. Love gone awry, amiss in sixty seconds. Quel dommage. There are only two love stories: those that succeed and those that fail. I am conversant in the latter. I can recite the alphabet of love, alpha to omega. We begin; we end. Alphabet soup. And I am not obtuse. I understand that one has to remove the mask to love, and I understand why this is difficult for me. Trust is not my strong suit. I learned at too young an age that men reify women, project onto them the masks they need to love. So a pedophile makes a lover of a toddler. I have laced myself, corseted myself into all sorts of shapes expected of me: trophy housewife, arm adornment, professional woman, sex goddess, WASP preppie. Enough. I just want to breathe. To be. I will no longer totter around on my high heels feeling like a hologram with legs. And the cost is great. I am more than a decade alone and suspect that the chance for love has slipped me by. I am too old perhaps.

Sometimes I feel like taking the sack off my head and screaming, "I am not an animal; I am a maintenance project." Exercise. Cosmetics. Hair dye. Contact lenses. Hair removal. Hair curlers. Wrinkle cream. Hydroelectric dams require less maintenance. Beauty and age oppose each other if you construct feminine beauty as I do. Fortunately, beneath the cosmetic mask I maintain remains a self with other impulses. I write. It staves off loneliness. And the mask will eventually crack; the time machine break down.

The Gilligans are getting boisterous and less little-buddy-buddy than they were on their arrival. Two of them are arguing about which float deserves first place. My corvine courter has rejoined her murder of crows. I prefer the exultation of larks. The acrobats from Rutland's Japanese sister city still chatter happily. I assume happily. They do not appear to suffer linguistic alienation as I do when I travel, but then they travel together. They are their own linguistic group. The crow ladies, ebon and caped, cackle in their coven on this night when souls tiptoe through the veils. Samhain. All Souls'. Martinmas. This mensal cusp. Halloween is my favorite holiday. The Celts believed in circular time. Samhain marked their New Year. How lovely once a year to become young again. This is a pagan evening of runes and cards, a clairvoyant night when the Wicked Witch can scry into her crystal ball. Autumn, my favorite time of year, when leaves scuttle like mice over the pumpkins, shadows dance through stubbled cornstalks, and stones develop souls and sing. An animistic world that blooms deep in my old druid blood.

I love the retablos of the Dia de Los Muertos, the gleeful clay skeletons attired in the uniforms of their trades. The streetwalkers tarted up in miniskirts and heels, the carpenters in their coveralls, the taxi drivers with their caps, all cheery, so happy to be dead. They seem far happier than their living counterparts.

Am I happy? I am not unhappy. Do I regret Carlo? No. He is another ellipsis in a long series of them. Okay, he did not turn out to be Lizzie Borden's stepbrother, but he was more Scaramouch than Casanova. The most beautiful masks I have seen hang in the storefronts in Venice—long-nosed harlequins and death masks and plague physicians' beaks like something from a Bosch painting, half-man, half-bird. Carlo was half-bird; he flew the coop before we even had a chance to roost, to nest, to nestle. But who could blame him? Not I. I turned out to be a Lizzie Borden understudy with coruscating bread knife and wine-smudged mouth, a demented Dionysus.

Lizzie Borden took a knife, But she took not a single life. When Carlo had come and gone, Lizzie Borden was alone.

I read that Lizzie Borden's former home in Fall River is now a B and B. *Who* would sleep there? That's more crossing over than I would like to do. A bed I could not lie in, and a breakfast I could not swallow. I doubt that the Borden skeletons grin. Only those who died violent, unresolved deaths, I suspect, remain on this side of the veil to haunt, much as only the unresolved loves linger. I have my unresolved loves, but I do not count Carlo's among them, too erumpent an exit. He is gone.

But I suspect that the Bordens abide. Abby and Andrew and Lizzie. Their last meal on August 4 in 1892: bananas, johnny cakes, and sugar cookies. How sweet.

On Samhain the Irish celebrate the feast of the dead with nuts and apples. The nuts associated with wisdom and the apple with the underworld, the afterlife. A balanced diet. Traditionally Samhain is a time of peace, a time to marry.

I scan the bar, but I see no likely marital prospects. I smile at a Gilligan, faute de mieux. Looking for love is like looking for your glasses without them when you have misplaced them. You can't see them because you can't find them. And truth? Men frighten me. I told a girlfriend, "Men give me the willies." She answered, "Women give men the woodies." I guess that sums it up. But it doesn't improve the conversations with the furniture. This is how life will break your heart.

Samhain is the evening when you can squint into the future. I see myself. I will be a knowledgeable crone, making gingerbread of small kinder and kinder of gingerbread.

I will be the dotty old lady who passes out sugar cookies to neighborhood children. I will die alone. We all die alone. On the other side I will be a wiggy, twiggy, jigging skeleton with stacks of paper notepads and small clay pens. Of this, I am unafraid.

Grown men in dog suits scare me. Goofy sensed this when I was in Disney World, so he stalked me. It unnerved me that a grown man would be willing to make his living wearing a dog costume and bobbling his head like an imbecile with a big nose and a stupid beribboned hat. And that horrible hyupping voice. And I knew he was in there, dammit, some grown man in Wholesomeland with his face obscured, leering at me, fleering at me, following me and relishing my uneasiness.

My pedophile wore a dog suit. He was a man inside a hound, a bloodhound. Wherever I go, he is the man who walks beside me, the interstitial presence.

The Irish have only two seasons, winter and summer. Liminal, Samhain marks their convergence and divergence. The evening when the fairy folk leave until Beltaine. On Samhain if you and your true love toss nuts onto the hearth and the nuts burn, then you shall endure. All of my nuts crack. It is time like the wee people to be leaving.

Closing time. I love Leonard Cohen's song with that title. The Irish have their own, "The Parting Glass." Its lyrics, anagogic for me. As I stand to leave, the three crows intercept me and pull me into their ring of hands, and for just a moment we twirl around giddily while the acrobats clap. Then I break from the ring and wave to the Gilligans. Goodnight, all, goodnight. And the leopard lady raises her parting glass. A cat mask drops on the floor.

I sing as I leave. "But since it falls unto my lot that I should go and you should not, I'll gently rise and softly call, goodnight and joy be with you all."

Abandoned Shoe

I opened a borrowed umbrella and a tiny slip of paper fluttered down. I recognized it. The printed fortune from a cookie shucked in a Chinese restaurant. But I was going to meet a train. I walked into the rain.

Later I thought about it. What was the likelihood that a fortune would land in a closed umbrella, abide there like a secret until the owner loaned the umbrella, only to open itself to the intended, only to open itself to the future on a day of openings in early June, when bud to blossom to leaf, I was going to meet a man in a train station and perhaps open myself to love again.

What might the fortune say? Roll over your IRA into your mutual fund? Check the valves on your front tires? Place twenty dollars on Grave Matter to win? Marry the guy at the depot? You are going to die alone?

Or some tautology? He who smiles is happy? A man in love is never poor. Rabbits tell no secrets. Every square has corners.

I met my guest and drove him back to my house, then searched the area around my stoop for the fortune. I found it on my bottom step, the ink bled to pink. No fortune. My future, bleached or tinted rosy? No message for me. A curtailed lifeline? Perhaps fortuitous after all. Such is my fortune.

I am what happens when you walk under ladders.

To resume the present: I meet my date at the depot. When he arrives, I kiss him. "Do you love me?" I ask him.

He says, "The Tokyo Zoo closes every year for two months so that the animals get a break from the tourists."

I take that for a NO.

The Depot. The station was built in 1924. A beautiful, old clock from a railroad station in Troy, New York, refuses to disclose the time on one wall. All time is present, fixed as its hands. Long benches line the room. A phone booth lined with tin stands like a sentinel's post, the phone within is out of order.

I, too, am out of order. I have an unruly heart.

In the nineteen-sixties my mother wore elbow-length gloves, black, with a mink-trimmed swing coat. The coat had a matching mink hat with a veil. I bought a similar pair of gloves because I wanted to know what they felt like. They feel elegant perhaps because they are so unnecessary, so frivolous, unfunctional. Perhaps because they are slinky. Perhaps because their presence emphasizes my bare shoulders and neck. The fingers of the glove feel as if they were meant to pinch a tapered ivory cigarette holder.

I was not able to find a hat with a veil. What is the meaning of the veil? That people on the other side of it need protection from the wearer's devastating beauty? Or is it the wearer who needs protection, her beauty too delicate for the common raucous round of daily life? Does looking through its filmy scrim much alter the world? Does the veil tat the world into lace? Or is it intended for audience, a drape of mystery? The almost glimpsed allure?

With the man in the depot I do not need a veil. He is not trying to love me. Protection is not required.

He tells me that when Jacques Lacan came to the United States, he believed himself to be famous. He was unknown. He asked his secretary to arrange a private tour of the Metropolitan Opera House. His secretary obliged by requesting a private tour for Jean-Paul Sartre who had some peccadillos, among them that he did not like to be addressed by name. The director was delighted to welcome the celebrity but not by name.

Knots fascinated Lacan in his later years. He loved the curly cords of American telephones and colored, plastic shower curtain rings.

I love elbow-length gloves and veils.

The man I meet at the depot loves magnetic shoes.

His name is Gregory. (That is not his real name but it has about it, something of the blue startle of his eyes.)

Gregory does not address me by name.

I meet Gregory in Bellows Falls, because he wants to go to Mass MoCA in North Adams. After we stop at my home, I drive him there. Route 2 winds through the Berkshires with its abandoned roadside cottages and motor courts. Tourist attractions from the thirties and forties still dot the route—oversized Indians standing columnar over tiny gift shops. Spindly wooden fire towers with foliage overlooks and hand-lettered signs, rusting mounted binoculars with quarter slots.

It seems an unlikely road to a contemporary museum. It is a road from another America, an earlier one, when cars and food were slow, and a vacation was a drive into the country, a stop and start procession of cars gawking at parti-colored leaves. Picnics, perhaps. Diners. "Seeing the sights," a quaint redundancy.

Now it is early June. The leaves are a pale green froth on the branches, lace. The grass is soft and a bright yellow-green. Little traffic. Weeds spring up in the parking lots of the gift shops and motor courts. The sky is a paler blue than Gregory's eyes, more forget-me-not than BlueGregory, with clouds scumbled against it. It would be a good day to be in love, but I have lost the capacity if not the inclination. That sadness thrums in me like a bass note. Deep, buried, always there, vibrating slowly.

I drive; Gregory tells me about Martin Heidegger, how the translation of *Sein und Zeit* which he liked best was by a kami-kaze pilot. It had the authenticity of death. Heidegger did not know that the translator was one of the last conscripts into the Divine Wind pilots, a fleet of children, the elderly, the feeble. His nearsighted translator missed the ship that was his target and crashed into the sea.

Gregory and I are both nearsighted. We are marking half a century. We knew each other in high school and recently, after thirty years, found each other again. Sea or ship, death is death. It always has authenticity.

Gregory squints at me. Actually he squints at everything. "You don't have any response to that? My Heidegger story?"

"It's interesting."

"Interesting?" he says in falsetto.

"Death is death."

"Deep," he says.

"Jung at heart," I say.

"Jung?" he asks. He rubs his palms on his denimed thighs. "You are the most unhip person I ever met."

I ignore him. Fight or flight. Jack be nimble; Jack be quick. Jack slip under limbic stick.

I am the sound of a spider on paper. I drive and think about how spring happens. The green buds like beads on branches, the tight curls of fiddleheads gradually unfurling into ferns. I wriggle in a happy animal moment.

"What are you doing?" he asks.

"Enjoying my environment."

"Environment?"

"Yes. Beautiful day. Adapting to the land. My brother told me that carp will always grow to the size of their environment, be goldfish in a bowl, catfish-sized in a pond, huge in a lake."

Gregory says, "Nah. If that were true the universe would be carp."

Gregory's universe is carp. He complains. About everything. Often. We are not different; we are opposite. He is urban; I am rural. He is broke; I am prospering. He is self-educated. I have more degrees than a thermometer. He has no family. I have a close one. It is a long list of antinomies. But we are both writers.

When Joyce met Yeats, he said, "We have met too late for me to have any effect on your poems."

Gregory and I have re-met too late for him to have any effect on my heart. But once we loved each other, once we loved each other so much that I left an egg boiling on the stove. We became otherwise occupied on the floor. While we were cavorting, the water boiled away. The egg exploded. It exploded loudly. It exploded widely. It exploded with enthusiasm.

Gregory says, "You've lost weight."

"You've heard of the Doctor Atkins diet?"

Gregory says, "Uh huh."

"I did the Doctor Demento diet. The all-stress diet." Men make me nervous.

Gregory stares out his window.

Ahead on the side of the highway is an empty shoe. A woman's high heel. Black. It defines loneliness. It begs for a story. It is tired of being inexplicable.

At MoCA I spend the most time in Robert Wilson's installation, "14 Stations," 2000. This enclosed small town with its stark New England cottages of light and sound enchants, haunts, disturbs. I want a new conversation with myself, and I find it in this vaulting warehouse of a room. The first station frightens me most, Jesus Condemned to Death, a well of horror, a well of sounds. I pause there because Jesus was thirty-three when he died. I will be fifty in January. My life is no longer what it will become; it is what it has been.

Little birds nest under my door stoop. At night a yellow egg of moon rises through the prismatic glass in my bedroom window. I hear the whispery scritches of batwings. Almost fifty I am trained to solitude. Only in public do I still feel like a ball made out of rubber bands, an outer band about to pop. The whole ball springing apart, bands zinging around the room. Me all over.

I am a highway heel, out of place, missing its mate.

The Hermeneutics of Abandoned Shoes: they always suggest violence to me. A woman raped or beaten, pushed from a moving car. Or a woman deserted by her date, left to walk midnight highways in stilt heels until a car sideswipes her. Headlights tangle in the trees. A thump. She leaves a shoe as she takes leave.

Once I found a pair of jeans on a dirt road. What upset me most was their size. They were tiny. A size two or four. Girl's jeans. They looked so forlorn that I eventually placed them inside a nearby abandoned cabin. They seemed in need of shelter.

In the museum, Gregory approaches me, walking down the long nave of the installation.

Wilson wrote of the piece, "I always work with a horizontal line, which stands for time, and a vertical line, which, for me, always means space. Time and space are two crossing lines, a structure that forms the architecture of everything." Gregory is a thin black line. The architect of everything. He walks through time and space. Behind him an arboreal apse resurrects itself, where a figure hangs upside down above a blue bed.

His eyes are blue beds. He does nothing more than squeeze my forearm and say, "Thanks." It is enough for the moment. It is enough. Our passionless Passion Play.

We drive back to my home, the conversation desultory.

The vertical line is the spatial line, the spiritual line. When I went to see Gregory in New York, we stayed in a borrowed townhouse. Gregory was cat-sitting for friends. Fur balls as large as tumbleweeds swirled in the corners of the townhouse. Laundry decorated every available surface—floors, tabletops, chairs, bureaus. Heaps of clothes everywhere. The bathroom ceiling was not. Leaks had removed it. Stripped the wallpaper, too. Toys took over the living room. Dirty dishes towered in the kitchen. The light was too poor to read. It sleeted every day. I balanced myself on the edge of a chair and stared blindly at book after book. Gregory was cranky and complained about the bad light, the weather, my containment.

On Day Three I made a discovery that redeemed it all. In a tumble of culch on a kitchen counter? Table? Bookcase? The surface was indiscernible. I found a dog-eared copy of a book, *Feng Shui*. Although I was alone in the townhouse, I rumbled into stomach-clutching laughter.

This housekeeper is worried about "wind-water"? About energy flow? If energy walked into this house it would bang its shins on the fur balls. Balance the yin and yang? Where? On the laundry? Chi in the house wouldn't have room to move. It wouldn't have room to turn around. A book on Feng Shui? This house needed a book on the uses of the vacuum cleaner.

But I was delighted. How not to be? It would be a little like a love manual on one of my bookshelves. Everyone needs to be inexpert at something. I fail at love.

We are home from the museum. Gregory is inside sleeping or reading. I am sitting on my little deck beneath a sift of stars listening to the coyotes ululate and yip. Gibbous moon. I can smell the lilacs, grapey and dark. My first kiss was in a lilac bush. Those heart-shaped leaves.

The olfactory sense resides in the limbic, old reptile brain. Above it in the old mammalian brain sit memory and emotion. The smell of lilacs is forever a first kiss. The smell of lilacs is love. A memory of love.

If we were offered our lives anew, would we repeat them or live them differently? I suspect that we would repeat them. Personality may be a form of stutter. Perhaps life is always preterite, some irrecoverable former self one longs to be again.

The door bangs open. Gregory stands there. "What you doing?"

"Thinking."

"What about?"

"The past."

"Baby," he says. "Don't. That's just waddling through porridge."

I laugh, then say, "Kiss me."

He does. Lightly. The kiss of distant relatives. No lilacs.

He pauses, studying me in the dark. He leans against the rail. "Say what it is you need to say," he says. "Your sensitivities can kill you."

But I do not need to say anything. It is early June. The season before fireflies. I can wait.

In the 1960s my mother wore a mink hat with a veil, a swing coat with three-quarter-length sleeves, trimmed with mink, and elbow-length gloves. I am thinking about the meaning of elbow-length gloves, how sleek they were, how one could only imagine how slowly they peeled off. A tug at the fingertips, an expression of bored hauteur, and then the long sequence of the glove, the forearm revealing itself.

The glove is time. The veil is space.

My hands are in my lap, ungloved. I wear my face. The lilacs smell like love. Beneath the stars, I'm in my place.

The Flying Rabbit and the Disappearing Playground

There's a man I can't forget. How many stories begin with that line? But this is not an unrequited love story. The man whom I can't forget gave me a pillowcase as a wedding gift, my first wedding. He was a country boy from a Vermont family, the sort of family that didn't live on Main Street or Church Street, but on a street closer to the places where you didn't want to be from, Dump Road or a road with no name that had a house that everybody in town said was haunted. But it was merely abandoned. For a long time. Too long. I don't know for certain which road he lived on. He lived on the periphery. Periphery Road. His name was Gray Dalton (my invention). And he was the sweet one, the good boy of the Dalton boys. Rusty, his brother, was a rock 'n' rolling, hard-drinking, skirt-chasing, wise-cracking, law-breaking, cuddlesome bundle of trouble. But Gray was sweet. He was cursed with niceness.

A mutual friend told me years later that Gray went crazy. He attended Julliard, studied classical guitar, graduated, returned to Vermont and kept setting fire to his apartments until he was institutionalized. Maybe his arsonist heart found it trying to be the good brother. Scorch that.

I recall Gray telling me that his mother had suggested the pillowcase. People always can use pillowcases, she said. But not this one. This was a single pillowcase in a shade of gold that would only match whatever had been purchased with it. This pillowcase would not go with white. It was a solo pillowcase, a gold pillowcase, a lonely pillowcase. It would never find a match. A pillowcase for a spinster's head. Why not two pillowcases? Surely Goldie deserved a groom. Two cases, two heads for the marital bed. But, no, one pillowcase.

At the time, I thanked Gray. I do not believe that I ever used that pillowcase, nor do I know what became of it. Nonetheless all these years later, that solitary, harvest-gold sham signifies for me. Gray intuited my future, I believe now. That marriage lasted not a year. My second marriage lasted fourteen. I am twice married, and I have never been loved.

This lovelessness rankles me more these days as time wrings its inexorable hands. I have looked out my bedroom window at the disappearing playground. The sandbox first. Then the swing set. Then the trampoline. My son just turned eighteen. I just turned fifty. I am menopausal and living alone in a town in the desolate southeastern corner of Ohio. I spend far too much time staring out windows. It is an expression of my claustrophobia, geographic, existential, mortal. I am the feeling of a bus passing through town.

On the train Ruth Kligman said to Edith Metzger, "Let your fantasy take over, make your wildest dream come true." Ruth Kligman lived. Edith Metzger, coming home from a party that she never attended, died on Firehouse Road on August 11th, 1956, around ten in the evening, north of East Hampton on Long Island in the Oldsmobile convertible that Jackson Pollock crashed into an embankment. These details pertain; they matter. I wanted to write Edith's story, the untold one, the arrested one. But I could not find any information on Edith, plenty on Ruth and Jackson. Those stories write themselves in brash letters, action-painted. What hopes did Edith have on that summer night? What party dress did she wear cinched at the waist like the stems of a nosegay clutched in a gloved debutante's hand? I am drawn to the covert stories, the ephemeral and unmourned players, the drama in the wings. For Edith, for me, no soteriological rescue, no divine hand writing a reprieve. Edith and I are holographs, written in our own hands. The page is quiet.

I can no longer have children. I am saying good-bye to my son. It feels like this: busybusybusybusygone. The *gone* is a precipitous drop. I find myself playing my life with my son backward like an old home movie in a projector, where swimmers splash out of the water and land neatly and dryly on the dock and everyone in the darkened living room laughs. The image ripples on a bed sheet pinned to the wall.

"Do you remember this?" I ask my son. "Were you happy then?" I ask these questions aloud. He is tolerant, a little amused. "Mom," he says, "I am going to college, not to another galaxy." He is wrong of course. This is a galactic shift, but I nod. He is trying to reassure me, and I need to let him do so. What I ask myself: how the hell did I ever pull this off—raising this beautiful child into a beautiful man by myself just south of the middle of nowhere?

By myself. This is how I do everything. Fifty is the great divide. I am no longer becoming who I am. I am become who I am, and who I am is cumulative—who I have been as well. I am slipping down the other side of the mountain now, the backside of the plot of my life, living my life in mirror time, reversed, memory, a curse. I find myself giving belongings away—sets of pottery, linens, hall runners, stereo systems, televisions, extra chairs. My seating plan is for one. I no longer collect antiques, curios. Fifty is the beginning of the years of divestiture.

Rusty Dalton snared all the girls. He lived for a while in a rickety hotel in Bethel, long since burned down. He would receive one lover at the hall door while another snuck down the fire escape. He wore jaunty caps, drank too much, and referred to women as "peaches." Did Gray watch all this and wonder, What do they see in him? *Peaches* date the bad boys, but, as we age, we seek the Grays. But they are long since locked in the asylums or long since happily married. Gold pillowcase. Gold band. Rusty died young in a car crash on his way home from a gig, wrapped his car around a sugar maple. His girlfriend of the moment, unlike Edith Metzger, walked away from the car. Dead at the wheel, Rusty was thirty-two.

There is no manual for this aging. No one prepares you for the declining energy, how your body betrays you, how haunted memory becomes, how it starts working overtime, the loss of impact when you enter a full room in a new black dress, the startle when you look in the mirror (Who is **that**?), the expense of the maintenance as the infrastructure collapses—hair, skin, exercise clubs, pedicures—the diminishing circle of friends, the bass note of sounding sadness in your life, *So this is it then?,* and the terrifying loneliness. Unprepared for all this—my son's leave-taking, the awareness that I will die alone, turning fifty, menopause—I came close to becoming A Girl Interrupted. But I cannot indulge the luxury of a breakdown. I am all I have. I fought back hard this time. From time to time I dismantle myself, perhaps so that I can build anew. But I keep constructing the same self. I need a new idea.

I do not give up. I check my e-mail daily hoping for a different message. I receive come-ons for Viagra, lower interest mortgage rates, increased penis size, special buys on meds, and foreign lotteries which I have apparently already won. It occurs to me that this is exactly what I need—me blissed out on an economical sedative, smug, with a full bank account, an affordable home, and my very own enhanced and generous erection. But that is life in Cyber-land. I delete the messages. Nonetheless I do not give up.

I paint my toenails pink. I try not to listen to Kate and Anna McGarrigle sing "No One to Turn Off the Lights." I lift furniture alone. I use lighter shades of lipstick. I wear silk panties only, French cut. I run up huge phone bills, phone bills commensurate to the Pentagon budget, speaking to friends, family long distance. Even when I sleep alone, I wear princess-seamed silk nightgowns. I sleep with a body pillow facing east. I scratch my own back, have a bootjack, a zipper pull, and a bracelet fastener, a programmable espresso maker. These keep me from feeling my aloneness too keenly. Now if only I could teach the coffee maker to bring me a cup in bed.

Perhaps we go through everything alone. I cannot know because I have never known love. I'd like to think that love, as I can imagine it, eases the solitariness. I did love a man once, but it was not returning in kind, in degree. The last time I spoke to him, he called me on the verge of sleep, my sleep not his. I no longer even know where he resides. He is as lost as Edith Metzger. He was, for a while, my male double, my bad brother, my mirror self. He is no longer located on the map of my heart. Latitude turned lassitude. Longitude become vicissitude. Now the ensuing stillness.

This winter in Ohio I became aware of all of the animal activity that I usually overlook, because we had snow for weeks, ground cover. I tracked the deer who were browsing inside my fence.

The skittish hops of birds near my feeder. The delicate tracks of squirrels and chipmunks. The exclamatory footprints of rabbits. The punctuation of what had been. How busy they all were, and this life had been invisible to me all the while. I am leading an invisible life now. No one marks me. I leave no tracks. Perhaps this is why I write this essay?

Last winter on sabbatical, I lived in Vermont, and we had great drifts of snow, snow to the window sashes, snow to the flower boxes, snow to the apple tree branches. Hyperborean, I love the snow and cold. Staring out the window as is my custom, I noted rabbit tracks, blue chevrons in the dazzling January sun, leading to the apple tree, but underneath it, they suddenly disappeared. Curious. I pointed them out to my brother, Danny. "How odd," I said. "That rabbit just disappeared as if it could fly."

Danny folded his arms and studied me. "You're not kidding, are you? What lovely logic. Joan, a raptor probably swooped down for rabbit brunch."

Oh. It never occurred to me that the rabbit had been scooped up. Little Rabbit Foo Foo. Hare today. Goon tomorrow. I prefer to live in a world of flying rabbits.

As the playground has been disappearing gradually, I have been having a recurrent dream about my father sitting in a rocking chair in a corner of our old summer home. The rocking chair is white and stands next to a washstand with pitcher and basin. Figured yellow wallpaper trellises the room, a water stain in the corner that looks like the head of a rabbit. The curtains, white Priscillas, billow blousily. Sometimes one of the dark-green roller shades, over-wound, snaps up suddenly while I nap. Then they come, the faces; the distorted goblin faces, wobbly, hungrily quiver through the window, and gobble my father. They take him away from me. I know what the dream means.

My father was all that rocked between me and a pedophile. I did not tell my father about my abuser, but I understood when I was a girl that my father was my protector. It was a child's dream, and it is recurring now because sometimes I wonder whom I might have become. I wish that I could rock myself back through time to that five-year-old girl, before sexual knowledge, before I became stunted and thwarted like some crabbed apple tree pushing out branches at erratic angles in order to see what other, lovelier woman I might have become, an apple tree in bloom in spring, upright, bridal in the orchard procession. Perhaps I still would have constructed this glorious, crotchety mess that I am today. Perhaps we are blueprinted to always raise the same house. Still I would like to know if some other residence might have been possible. But with my too-early knowledge of men I began to construct a house of barbed wire, guile, wit, broken bottle glass, fear, outsider art, outsider architecture. I learned that what men say is different from the idiom of their eyes. In the hands of my tutor, I became fluent in cruelty. I live in a haunted house. Perhaps we all have a bad brother, the damaged twin who resides with us, in us. We struggle to see who will get mastery of the house, the terrified cellar dweller, pale as a potato tuber, the attic keeper, surveying the land, eyes solemn, from her objective altitude.

(But I have been loved. By my father. Invisible tracks in snow.)

I was fortunate to hear the poet Robyn Schiff speak about the haunted house of authorship. For women, I suspect, the house is always Gothic, the edificial always an externalization of the psychological. When our homes are in order, we are in order. When we decorate the rooms of our homes, we are always in-terior decorating, the ulterior interior, the self with all its hallways and doorways and secret passageways and subterranean chambers. I love my homes, both of them, my house in Ohio filled with New England antiques, and my camp in Vermont, a converted barn with a cupola that oversees the comportment of the mountains, Killington, Salt Ash, and the ring beyond, their winter stark majesty, their spring green playfulness, their autumn riotousness, and cloud-scudded summer blues, the circadian play of tilting light.

But in the two settings, I am more myself, most myself in Vermont. As I swept my kitchen this Vermont June morning, I thought about the gaps in the plank pine floors. I will always haunt this house. My hair always nestled mouse-like into the chinks, my skin mottling the dust, long after I am a flying rabbit. My camp, a converted barn, lacks a cellar. It sits on rock ledge and stilts of timber. I am glad for this, the cellar a dark place in my psychic architecture, a door the child slams shut against her pedophile who used to lure her there with promises of root beer. The root beer came later, after the tussle, the measled magazines, the smell of potatoes rotting, of rust, mold, stale sweat, rancid tobacco. I do not like the descent into cellars. I like above stairs, homes honeyed with light, yellow light, pretty light.

I will not go down those stairs again. I'd rather be a flying rabbit.

These two homes compose myself, Vermont and Ohio. I am my own good sister and bad sister, my own Gray and Rusty. What I most fear is myself, losing myself, my good self, stumbling, pitching headlong down those stairs to the cellar landing, legs and arms broken, unable to crawl back into yellow light. I could root in that despair and never find the lowest stair, the first stair. What I fear most at fifty: my son's departure. Who now, what now makes me rise up out of myself? What aspect of light awaits me at the top of the stairs? How will I stop haunting myself?

My writer friend, Joe, and I go on adventures in Vermont, spook around the state, trying to scare up stories to write. In the western part of the state, almost on the New York border, on a griddle-hot July day, we found a neglected little corner of the county and followed a road alluringly, promisingly marked Ghost Hollow Road. It wound along a river, murky and sluggish, so sluggish that it could be wallowing top to bottom with flopping catfish rather than running with water. It looked like a place that belonged somewhere else, Alabama, maybe, Mississippi, and some time else, forty years ago, maybe fifty. Along the dirt road, abandoned campfires smoldered. Makeshift lean-tos and tents, transient encampments with heaps of burned tin cans and weather-crumpled clothing, dotted the wayside. Occasionally some dinged-up old Ford or Chevy, finned and ruthless, rust-hungry for the road, winked its walleyed headlights at us as we idled past. But the smoldering fires bothered me. We did not see a single person, but the fires suggested sudden leave-taking. I felt that the forest beamed with eyes. Eyes behind every maple. Eyes behind every birch. The roadside forested with eyes. Despite the July heat, I shivered. The sooty, slender plumes of smoke curled sinisterly. Evasiveness, elusiveness, we were in the land of the *un*found, the *don't want to be found*. The smoke smelled like burned garbage, wet, organic. The heaps of discarded clothing hunched, somehow criminal, violent. I thought, Vagrant. Tramp. Hobo. Hobo, a quaint, antiquated word, but this Ghost Road, a place set in some interstice of time, contemporized the word. A blur, something, someone big, bolted across the road in front of Joe's car. My heart did a Bigfoot lurch. "Roll up your window," Joe said. And I did. We rolled on through the creepy hobohemian settlement until we came to a bridge and swerved onto a road, tar, more recognizably set in Vermont and in this decade, this century, this millennium.

The Flying Rabbit and the Disappearing Playground 133

Hobo. Etymology uncertain. Ho, beau? Ho, boy? Hobos evolved their own language of symbols to rate the jails, to warn each other off certain farmhouses, or about unfriendly police.

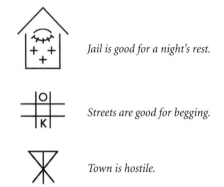

Jail is good for a night's rest.

Streets are good for begging.

Town is hostile.

The ideograms look like avian prints in snow. The bird scritches encrypting hieroglyphs I could not decode in the winter drifts. Only *we have been here. See. We have been here.* Like the hobos encoding their anonymous messages to each other, and perhaps that is enough. "See?" I say to you. "I have been here, too."

In Ohio, the snow melted, and the habits of birds became invisible again, the coterminous world of deer and rabbit and chipmunk and mouse. But for a moment, for a few days, they all left messages. "Present," they said. "Presence." Precious presence. Then the snow melted.

We all write in invisible ink.

My friend Joe also told me about the Beltane Phallus, an alleged Celtic ruin near Green Mountain Village. But the phallus fascinated me less than its analogue, Venus of the Snows, his neighbor. The phallus, while quite mimetic (albeit exaggerated) with its stone pileus, did essentially what all phalluses do;

it poked up. But Venus of the Snows ensorcelled, charmed, a lissome torso turning as if to meet a partner in dance. But the name most enchanted me. Venus of the Snows. The goddess of love, snowbound. What footprints has she overseen these many centuries? Her Beltane lover, rock-bound, fixed. He belonging to May, spring giving way to summer. She, the goddess of hoarfrosted love, wearing an ice-tatted veil. The two committed to never couple, ever be imminent, meeting. Why their proximity? To torture them with longing for completion, coition, or did they guide early Celts through some animistic ritual of male and female? Does rock feel? Do we raise rock to make our unendurable longing durable?

Disarming and disarmed Aphrodite of blizzards, stellar stela, I understand your position. It is my own. I, too, am a Venus of the Snows. Winter is my temperament, and cold is my climate. Around me the winter trees startle and release flocks of flying rabbits. See how they swoop and circle. The hawks whistle with misgiving. The deep woods, waist deep, shoulder deep in snow, wait, disquiet. Venus of the Snows, in her forested silence, hears brittle twigs, snap, drop and disappear into the powder, leaving behind their insignia. Venus of the Snows watches chance compose her calligraphic billet doux in the powder. Deep in the woods, she sings her melancholy love songs. She has been singing them for centuries. She has the carriage of a woman who once was beautiful. Beauty is evanescent. But not aspect. She has presence yet. She reclines on the bed(rock) awaiting her lover.

I was two years old when Edith Metzger died. With petrifaction, I, too, could be ageless.

Last April I stood on a lakeshore. Spring still promissory, the lake rippled gray, and last season's cattails rattled. I was strange in the sublime landscape like a figure daubed into a Hudson River School painting. Not a fisherman or a boater near. The camps huddled into the fallow fields, the leafless woods around the lake, windows darkly blinking, doors shuttered. The lake camps: unlit lanterns. Near an island, two wood ducks paddled and fished. I recalled what my last lover had said, "No man is a mainland," an inverted trope. My loneliness was exquisite then. Beholding such cold, unpeopled beauty, I felt like the last of a species. I walked along the shore. The intermittent sun sparked something in the thatchy grass. Everywhere shards of a broken mirror, jags of glass. What accident had happened here? Seven years' bad luck dating to what origin? My eyes here. A lip. My wind-chapped cheek. My hand reaching for a fragment. I populated the grass. Me all over. Not twinned, shattered. And I could not put the jigsaw together because every mirror fragment shape-shifted, eye, nose, hand, as I tried to reconstruct myself. I left the mirrors reflecting sky, sky, sky. Mirrors on the beach. Mirror time.

Toward the end, my last lover stamped my letters to him: RE- TURN TO SENDER. They boomeranged to me, unopened, unread. Homing pigeons, flying rabbits. Once he returned my letter to me in a fresh envelope, addressed in his hand (read, I presume) with a pink slip enclosed, "We wish you luck placing your material elsewhere." Mirrors on the beach.

My former in-laws lived on the beach, Sanibel Island. They took my husband and me ocean dredging, scooping up sea cucumbers and starfish, and sea horses. I had never seen a sea horse before, and they are delicate, almost transparent, with a crenellated spine. With balletic grace, they propel with their fins, bobbing and wafting, their sensitive equine faces forward looking. Their tails curl like pinkies around sea grass, anchoring them. Their fragility charmed me. They sing when they mate, and the male of this otherworldly species bears the children. Anthropomorphizing them perhaps, I found this noble, progressive.

My mother-in-law kept the sea horses. I pled, "Let's put them back." Sea, their element.

And she laughed. "Oh, you're sensitive. You want to free them just like my friend, Dotty."

Yes, I did very much.

She brought the sea horses home and put them in shallow dishes of bleach in the sun until they died.

Each tiny flip and splash of the sea horses' agony pained me. Some deep empathy in me rubbed me as raw as a knuckle on a grater. I asked her, please, to spare them.

She laughed and said, "I am **not** a vegetarian."

Then put a cow in bleach.

Unable to bear it, I retreated to the guest room and closed the door.

In the afternoon, she took the dead horses to the jeweler's where she had them gilded to wear around her neck. Her necklaces were gallows.

Gallows humor. This is the only way to confront fifty. Half Mae West, half Eeyore. As Lily Tomlin said, "Things are going to get a lot worse before they get worse." But my wit tends more toward the antic, impish. Now, for example, I am imagining those hobos hobnobbing in the hoosegow and rating the accommodations like AAA for indigents. Jail food no good:

N ... G   *Jail food is no good.*

One star. One starfish. The hobo trains, the iron horses, do not waft and delicately float. They roar and snort to their own schedules.

What would I like? To be wholesome and lithesome and toothsome and winsome but not fulsome or loathsome or gruesome. I would like to find love, to turn a head rather than just a phrase. But this chance is lost to me, empty as a gold pillowcase. Winsome? Lose some. Helen Hayes said, "The hardest years in life are those between ten and seventy." She was seventy-three years old.

Emmeline Leboeuf still received suitors in her boudoir when she was seventy-four years old, among her admirers, Maurice Chevalier, Jean-Paul Sartre, Marshall Petain. She married her husband Georges Boudoir when she was in her teens and took his name. But the *boudoir* took its name from her and her habit of receiving callers from the Parisian demi-monde in her private chamber. Flowers and lace and pillows and parasols, bunches of lavender and fine linens bedeck my boudoir. But le lit is empty. Odd that in French the bed is masculine; it seems such a feminine place—soft, rustling, the site of dreams.

As I am writing this, I glance out of the window over my desk and see my son studying his old tree house. What site of dreams is that perch for him? What memories does it raise in the imagination?

In Ohio the interior dominates. My New England antiques creating a metaphor for home. In Vermont the exterior dominates; my rooms open doors onto the beauty of the world out there— its rocks and mountains and birches, its purple light.

(Post)face. If prefaces are composed after work is written, then why are they *pre*faces? To speak beforehand. All speaking is beforehand in this endless negotiation of past and future. Behindhand is an epitaph. Composition is consciousness in time. This composition is a jeremiad, a lament about aging. Time is a juggernaut. But the jeremiad could give way to jubilee. Fifty may prove to be my recrudescence. What next having been a care-taker all my life, of husbands (2), of rabbit (1) nonflying, of cats (1 and 1 stray), of dogs (1 and 2 strays), of students and girlfriends and boyfriends and unhappy teens (uncountable) and, for eigh-teen years, my son (1 and only)?

Recently here in Vermont a doe attacked a young boy. His calves bore deep bruised hoof marks. When the boy's mother, upon hearing her child's screams, went to his aid, the deer threat-ened her. Mother to mother. She whisked the child inside and called the game warden who theorized that the doe must have a fawn nesting nearby that she was protecting. I sympathize with both mothers. I no longer bleed monthly, but I am hemorrhag-ing love. What is the tourniquet for this love, this imminent loss?

This morning while running I happened upon a doe and her fawn and not wishing to risk getting hooved to death, I U-turned. A quarter mile along, a mother partridge hustled her chicks across the road and created a diversion with feathery fluster when I neared.

Last year Jessica the cow died. She was famous for charming a moose, media-named, Josh, who became her lovesick com-panion. Originally the story gave me hope. If a cow can love a moose, then anyone could find love, even I. A cow is not the most elegant of animals, but a moose is a ragged patch of midnight, all snout and preposterous legs, and shaggy ungainliness. But af-ter seventy-six days of courtship, the long-spurned moose went back to where moose come from. Nineteen eighty-six, the year that my son was born. The red-ribboned Jessica hid from him in the pines, where moose's antlers cannot go, playing hard-to-get. My fancy is that she mourned him later. Girls need an object, a subject for love. Optimistic moose, girls get notional. I suspect that she grieved you as she died.

What do females do when there is no longer anyone to love? Love has been my vocation. Love measured in the diurnal round of chores, meals cooked, kitchens cleaned, clothes washed, pressed and folded, the haircuts and bandages, and art lessons, and school papers, and teacher conferences, and orthodontic appointments, the valentines and groceries, the dates, and little grievances, the large joys, the rides to and from. So we mark our devotions. I hope that I can bring that devotion now to writing. Bette Davis said, "Old age ain't no place for sissies." Neither is writing. Maybe now my good sister-self can set about the serious enterprise of writing and push the bad sister down the stairs, burn the bad sister with an arsonist's heart. Perhaps I can now learn to bear an empty white chair rocking. Perhaps a bleached cow can yet fall in love with an unnamed moose. Fly, rabbits, fly. Canter, (see)horses, canter. I have a decade left or two or three to find the Gray in me, to write calligraphically these, my scritches on snow. If no one reads them, they are yet composed.

Tolstoy's Daughter

When I was in grade school, my father and I used to go for daily walks. During the walks, we discussed many subjects—his feelings about his Irish heritage, his belief in nature's divinity, his fear about the inexorable nuclear fate of this world. I knew from our topics that my father took my intellect seriously, more seriously than I did. On these walks, I learned how to read my father, how to decipher his reactions as I inquired about God, identity, coincidence, infinity. His arched brow and carefully modulated tone of voice communicated both pride at my precociousness and tolerance of my ingenuousness: Ah, yes, he had been that sophomoric once, naive enough to believe in ultimate answers, young enough to marvel at large concepts: infinity, destiny, eternity.

As my father undoubtedly anticipated, my interest in these topics dwindled. Unfortunately the frequency of our walks also declined; during my late adolescence, we indulged them less often as my thoughts turned more sharply on the boyfriend du jour. But my memory of our walks and their importance to me refuses to fade. I can no longer recall the names of the boyfriends, but I still feel with a pang, a puncture like a broken rib, the first time that my father declined a conciliatory invitation from me to take a walk.

A walk. Sometimes birches. "I like to think some boy's been swinging them. But swinging doesn't bend them down to stay." A walk. The story of his Irish father, how he finally acknowledged his son's accomplishments with a crablike conversational scuttle: Cannon at the pharmacy said to me the other day, "You must be awfully proud of your son. "A long pause that could mean almost anything and did. Then: I answered him, "Yes, I am." A walk. Perhaps a reflection on the quality of the hay matted beneath our feet by a bedding frost. Perhaps just a moment of shared pleasure in a sunset which we elected not to describe but enjoy. A walk. My father's exploration of the meaning of a life's arc which is always unfinished by its very nature. A walk. It tends to take the shape of a thought. Or loneliness. Or love. They may, all three, equate.

I suspect that my walks with my father were walks through the fairy-tale forests of our fear. We connected on the path of our intersecting loneliness; wearing a red-cloak disguise or a wolf's sheepskin, it still was love. I betray myself, confiding this much ignorance, but, in my overripe middle age, I know only three incontrovertible truths—death, love for the family I was born to and the son who was born to me, and regret about the suspension of walks with my father.

I remember less and less about the conversations. But I find myself startling from sleepless dreams with details in high relief —the beach glass we collected, Dad favored the cobalt, it was rare; the heart-shaped leaves of a lilac hedge; the feathery brush of pampas grass; the chuddering marks of snowmobile trails we traversed on cross-country skis. We even walked on water, laughing as we goofed around on a pedal boat in the sober shadow of the Grand Tetons. The rocks in the water glittered, periwinkle blue, salmon pink, barn red. Details, but the conversations elude me. I do, however, remember one consistent theme. Dad often tried to communicate to me how he valued these walks with me as Tolstoy valued his privileged relationship with his daughter. Tolstoy's wife Sonia was a putative harridan and he found solace and refuge in his closeness to his daughter. I esteemed this conferral of preference. I probably reveled in it in some all too obvious Electral pattern. I also remember feeling unworthy, knew that I was worthy of neither my father's intelligences nor his intelligence. I was overreaching. I also felt traitorous in accepting that, by analog, I had typecast my mother as a nag. I was too literal. My mother was clearly no shrew. I, no saint. I suspect now that my father merely meant to suggest that he needed some escape from the quotidian routine, a walk away from the familiar and familial into the larger world, from the anteroom that was our home into the adjoining vaulted hall where all became possible. It took me a while to grasp that my father was only strolling, not fleeing. He was a flaneur, not a philanderer.

But in boarding school, I recall browsing through Bartlett (the dilettante's bible) and encountering these Tolstoy lines with perplexity: all happy families resemble one another; every unhappy family is unhappy in its own fashion [*Anna Karenina*]. I confess that during my adolescence, I encountered everything with perplexity. Nevertheless, some questions nagged me.

Were we an unhappy family? We were not, I decided. We were, against all odds, a happy family with a deep dose of doom, a tolerance for peccadillos, the usual respect for sibling lethality, and a preference for acerbic wit over pure meanness when we needed to make a point. Were we happy? Let's face it—family gatherings were a trial. We usually indulged some hyena-pitched, panicky laughter at our foibles as a family. But never, never have we doubted that we loved each other. Ah. But—as my adolescent perplex well knew—love is not happiness. True. But in three rounds out of four, love bested happiness, pinned it to the mat.

Unhappy families, the uniqueness of unhappy families, each to its own fashion—it is a quotable quotation, a memorable line. Pithy. Succinct. It is also completely fallacious. Sentiment fosters the general, the epigrammatic. Emotion is always specific and private, ineffable. This realization required years of experience and two failed marriages, what my mother terms The School of Character Building. The title redeems suffering.

Another consequence of believing myself to be the doppelganger of Tolstoy's daughter is that I have never read Tolstoy. I confess this with the abjection with which one should confess that one has never had a thought, even a stray one. But I could not read Tolstoy because it would qualify my walks with my father, and my walks with my father would qualify Tolstoy. I admit this deficiency with embarrassment, even rue, but I take comfort in a remark that a colleague recently made to me, "What I haven't read would constitute at least two entirely literate people."

In the shadow of my literary confessional, I pray to be forgiven: I have not read Tolstoy. Not *War and Peace*, not *Anna Karenina*. Perhaps as Alexandra learned, there are things one need not know about one's father. And need not know about one's daughter. That is why we stopped walking when I was around sixteen. Now that I am in my forties, my son walks with my father. From the long windows in the living room, I watch them chatter off down the dirt road. I watch them with envy as I sit not reading Tolstoy.

Over the last two months, however, that envy has transubstantiated into gratitude as I have resumed my walk with my father in an entirely unanticipated way. I was in the middle of moving into my new house in Ohio when my mother called to say that my father had been diagnosed with cancer. I left before my suitcases knew that they were packed. Thirty-two years ago my father had had cancer. The prognosis was dire. The old fear surged back. Fourth grade fear. The walking fear, the fear that no one would ever take me seriously again, that the source of my love and loneliness would disappear. What would be left me? Not-love? Not-loneliness? How much did the presence of my father define me, give me a shape which I could inhabit?

I have always felt mortal, and it causes me no anxiety except for my son. But I have assumed for many years that my parents are immortal. Like Greek gods, they live in the pantheon on the hill, raising hell, arranging destinies, holding sway over the antics of my world.

I drove for fourteen hours straight, my lap a greasy crumble of road food. I arrived unexpected to a dark house, my soul elating at the approach with each rut in the road. Their house. My home. Home. My moral center. My eyes needed to verify empirically that they were still here. I opened the door to swoon with familiarity.

What is it about imminent loss that makes even the most irritating habits endearing? On the kitchen counter I found three empty red candy foils. Throughout the house I found the wadded paper towels which my father always left behind, the half-drained water glasses, the discarded newspaper, catalogues, fans of discarded magazines and unopened envelopes. In the dark, I was stalking my father by his habits, tracking him by his litter from room to room — den to kitchen to library to greenhouse — only to return to the three red chocolate foils on the counter: so vulnerable, I thought my heart would break. I pulled my cardigan tight around me. Waiting for dawn, I wept.

I similarly wept when I saw my father in postsurgery. He had suffered a postoperative heart attack. Lying on the gurney, he looked like an empty foil. I had the good sense not to let him see me cry. My mother identified it as relief. I knew it was terror, terror at my selfishness, terror at his feebleness. Why did I always feel as if the emotions of others radiated around me in rims and spokes? Why did I never feel what I was supposed to feel, what others appeared to expect of me? I was ashamed of myself. But I found self-forgiveness in this — my father was a large, thoughtful man designed to move through forests with long strides, over frosty hills in high gear, down city blocks at a know-where-I'm-going gait. He did not belong on monitors, on machines and beds with wheels, dependent on buzzers and nurses and frenzied bouts of beepers, chest-thumpers, needles, alarms. He should be the source of activity not its object.

He came home from the hospital just a few days before my mother was scheduled to go in. I would be responsible for my father's care during recovery. The home health aide tutored me. She taught me how to put on his embolism stockings, switch catheter bags, empty them, sterilize them, how to monitor the meds. She instructed me on procedures in the event of every conceivable post-op disaster. This education did not calm me. I fainted once. When my brother picked up my mother, as I watched them depart, I felt the same inadequacy, the same desolation that I felt when I first left the hospital with my son: am I equal to the task?

I was more a Florence Nightmare than a Nightingale. I had no tolerance for gore and little patience. My father had lost his voice and could not communicate above a whisper. Because of the staples in his stomach, he could dress in nothing more substantial than a hospital gown. His first day home was the easiest. He was too weak, too drugged, too pained to acknowledge his care with anything other than a wounded animal gratitude. Pride had not yet cut him.

Day two got off to a dubious start. I went to roll on his embolism stockings, which have the elasticity and give of granite. My father eyed me skeptically. We do not touch each other except in greeting, leave-taking, or natural disasters. I don't think I had even seen my father's naked legs since he took me swimming at Star Lake three decades ago. He was as enthusiastic about my putting on his stockings as I was. "Call Danny," he whispered. I did. But I still had to tend to his other care. My brother was not about to play nurse. For six hours, my father and I endured the new intimacy with a barely contained embarrassment that bordered on hysteria until he emerged from the bathroom, stricken and gray. "What's wrong?" I asked.

I thought he was going to cry. I knew that I could not bear it if he cried. "I bled all over the bathroom. I don't want to disgust you. But I can't bend." Whispers.

"Oh, Dad. Nothing you do can disgust me."

I got him to bed and I cleaned up the bathroom.

The next morning he let me put on the embolism stockings. He shook his head, whispered, "No dignity."

I told him that I understood, but he was wrong. He had tremendous dignity. We had found it in mutual respect for each other's dignity. From our regard for each other's essential privacy, we stumbled into a newfound intimacy.

I watched my father's progress with quiet solicitude. Using a wooden rack as a walker, he began to get about the house, incrementally taking over more of his care—meals, disinfecting the hose, switching the bags, popping the meds. I kept a careful distance. I had to be close enough to hear an emergency whisper, distant enough to give him room for his convalescence. True, the bags, bandages, odors of alcohol, iodine, illness, urine, tweaked me with sudden mortal sadness, but the pangs were mainly empathic. I wanted my father again as he saw himself, restored to the physical competence, the rugged health, the restlessness of body and mind.

My mother came home, doubling the duty, but I only found the lesson of care reinforced. You achieve a matter-of-factness because you must. I finally understood nurses, that attitude which I mistook, misread as a generic response to the faceless masses of the maimed and ill. On the contrary, the attitude is elegant, stylized, the only attitude possible as one struggles to redress mortality, cope with its messes. Only the humanity of the patient pertains. The nurse's personality disappears beneath her uniform. It is a self-effacing act of kindness, not a detached efficiency. I had had it wrong for years.

One afternoon I heard the front door slap, and I looked out the window. I saw my father walking on the terrace, looking out at his patch, his small mountain kingdom. I knew then that he would be okay for now. Even though he could not speak, I knew that he was happy, happy with pure animal reflex, glad to be here on this perfect July day. Watching him, I knew that I was walking with my father.

The metaphor collapsed. He was not Tolstoy. I was not Tolstoy's daughter. I watched him with satisfaction as he drank in the day—the yellow light, the white clouds scumbled against the blue sky, the wind tattering the birch leaves. Now I could begin, begin at last to read *Anna Karenina*, *War and Peace*. I was walking with my father, and I'd walk the walk until we lost the path.

Winners of the
River Teeth Literary
Nonfiction Prize

Five Shades of Shadow
Tracy Daugherty

The Untouched Minutes
Donald Morrill

*Where the Trail Grows
Faint: A Year in the Life
of a Therapy Dog Team*
Lynne Hugo

The World Before Mirrors
Joan Connor